MICHAEL WAUGH
SHADOW BANKING (FCIR, PART 3), 2015
INK ON MYLAR
25 x 25"
COURTESY OF THE ARTIST AND VON LINTEL GALLERY

THE MIT PRESS

FELT TIME

The Psychology of How We Perceive Time

Marc Wittmann

translated by Erik Butler

"A fascinating and engaging tour of the psychology of time. The insights Wittmann provides into our complex relationship to time gradually build up to an intriguing and sometimes surprising picture, on which our experience of time holds the key to everything from making good decisions to living a fulfilled life."

—**Christoph Hoerl**, Professor of Philosophy, University of Warwick

HOW GAMES MOVE US

Emotion by Design

Katherine Isbister

"... an invaluable guide to the many ways that games can be designed to provoke powerful positive emotions, not to mention chills, goosebumps, and transformative experiences that change how we see ourselves and the people we play with. It's an essential read for all game scholars and game designers who want to make a real emotional impact with their work."

—**Jane McGonigal**, PhD, author of *Reality Is Broken* and creator of SuperBetter

Playful Thinking series

DOCUMENTARY ACROSS DISCIPLINES

edited by Erika Balsom and Hila Peleg

Artists, filmmakers, art historians, poets, literary critics, anthropologists, theorists, and others investigate one of the most vital areas of cultural practice: documentary.

Copublished with the House of World Cultures/ Haus der Kulteren der Welt (HKW), Berlin

ADJUSTED MARGIN

Xerography, Art, and Activism in the Late Twentieth Century

Kate Eichhorn

"... a marvelous media archaeology of the copy machine and the subcultures that proliferated around it over the last fifty years, a profound meditation on the fate of the 'recently outmoded' in the age of digital replication, and a toolbox of strategies for activists working with the weird materiality of copies today."

—**Marcus Boon**, York University; author of *In Praise of Copying*

THE MAGAZINE

edited by Gwen Allen

The artist's magazine as a place where new ideas and forms can be imagined and created, from the eighteenth century to the twenty-first.

Documents of Contemporary Art series
Copublished with Whitechapel Gallery, London | Not for sale in the UK and Europe

QUEER

edited by David J. Getsy

Key artists' writings that have influenced and catalyzed contemporary queer artistic practice.

Documents of Contemporary Art series
Copublished with Whitechapel Gallery, London | Not for sale in the UK and Europe

mitpress.mit.edu

LOS ANGELES REVIEW OF BOOKS QUARTERLY JOURNAL | SPRING 2016

COVER ART
ALEXIS SMITH
ICE, 2014
MIXED MEDIA COLLAGE
12 1/4 X 11 3/8"
COURTESY OF THE ARTIST
IMAGE COURTESY HONOR FRASER GALLERY
PHOTO JOSHUA WHITE/JWPICTURES.COM

The Los Angeles Review of Books is a 501(c)(3) nonprofit organization. The *LARB Quarterly Journal* is published quarterly by the Los Angeles Review of Books, 6671 Sunset Blvd., Suite 1521, Los Angeles, CA 90028. Submissions for the *Journal* can be emailed to EDITORIAL@LAREVIEWOFBOOKS.ORG. Visit our website at WWW.LAREVIEWOFBOOKS.ORG.

The *LARB Quarterly Journal* is a premium of the LARB Membership Program. Annual subscriptions are available. Go to WWW.LAREVIEWOFBOOKS.ORG/MEMBERSHIP for more information or email MEMBERSHIP@LAREVIEWOFBOOKS.ORG.

Distribution through Publishers Group West. If you are a retailer and would like to order the *LARB Quarterly Journal*, call 800-788-3123 or email orderentry@perseusbooks.com.

To place an ad in the *LARB Quarterly Journal*, email ADSALES@LAREVIEWOFBOOKS.ORG.

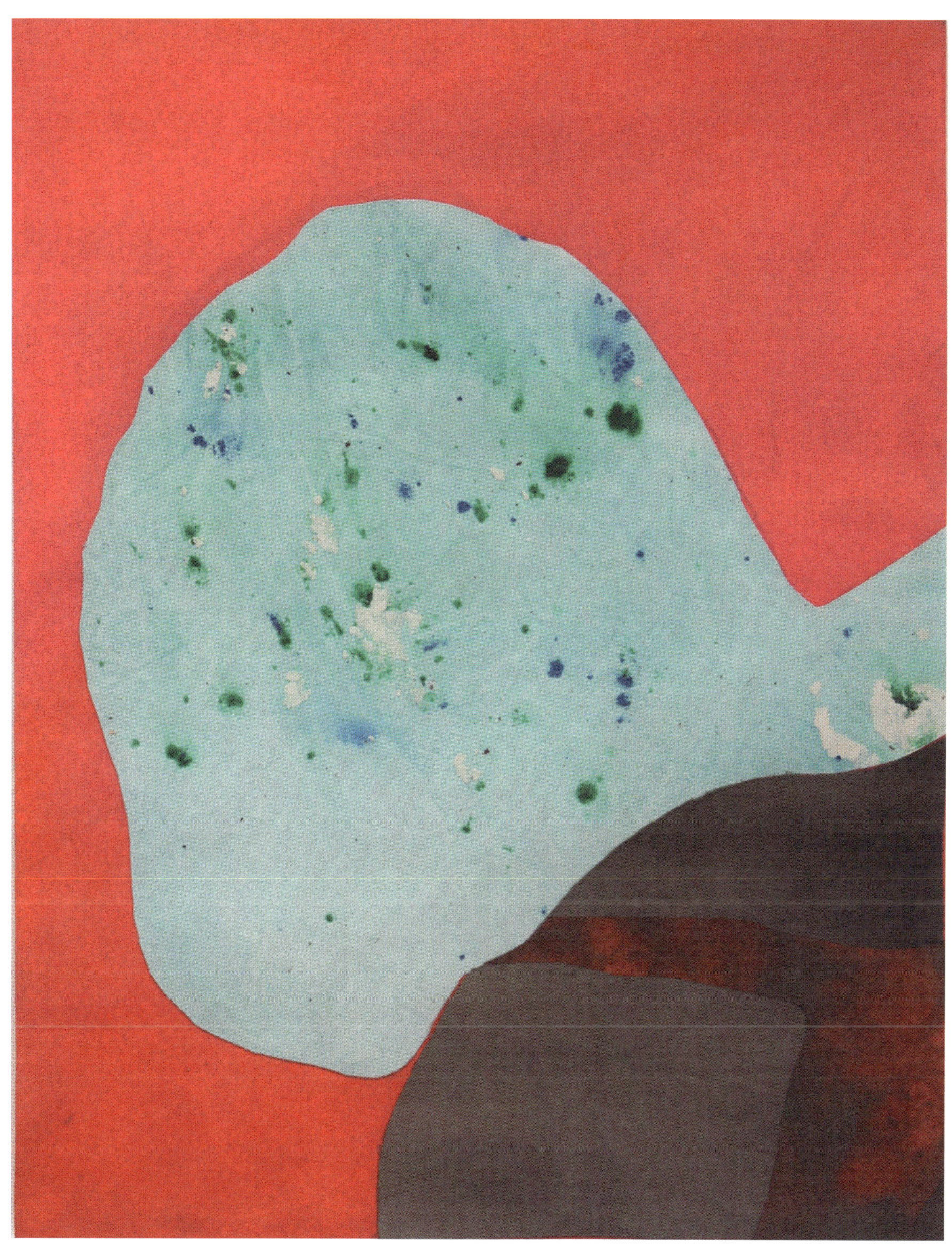

ALIKA COOPER
UNKNOWN #7, 2016
VINYL PAINT AND FABRIC ON PANEL
18 X 14"

PAT O'NEILL
UNTITLED (ROSEBOWL), 1968
GELATIN SILVER-PRINT, FRAMED
4 X 6"
COURTESY CHERRY AND MARTIN, LOS ANGELES
PHOTO: BRIAN FORREST

CONTENTS

THE BEST LITTLE WAR HOUSE IN MALI

ANNE JOLIS

This essay is a work of memory; there are no composite characters or compressed events. Names have been changed or omitted to protect the guilty.

THERE IS A HOTEL in northern Mali, just outside the center of a town called Gao. I can't tell you the name, though it wouldn't help you if I did. The hotel has no web presence, no mention on any map or guide. You'd have to go to Gao to find it, and I don't recommend that you do.

But if you do go to Gao, I guarantee you will find it. This is the only hotel in Gao. This is the hotel that the Qaedas allowed to stay open.

It has 12 rooms, clay and cement-brick, each with a four-poster bed, a side table, and *en-suite* plumbing. The rooms encircle a courtyard set with tables and chairs, and are protected by iron-barred windows and a blast-proof outer wall. Meals and coffee are not included, but a room for the night — 20,000 francs or about $35 — comes with security: four Malian soldiers clutching Kalashnikovs occupy the front gate at any given time.

There is no internet, not anywhere in Gao, unless you've brought a glowing Orange wi-fi stick that survived the drive up. But electricity snaps intermittently throughout the hotel during the day. At night, the owner's son Omar cranks a fatigued generator to life for a few hours. The generator retaliates by shocking one in six comers to its power cord.

Omar and his father are religious men, devout even by northern standards. If you pay your bills and bum a cigarette to Omar, he will ignore whatever booze you've brought onto the property. Not so the soldiers, who hail mostly from down south where the beer and the Islam both run freer. The soldiers, if they catch you with booze, will expect you to share.

Around the back of the main building, in which Omar keeps the hotel's books and the generator and three teenage servant girls in a small kitchen, a replacement shift of soldiers sleep in the gutter. Omar supplies them with sheets, but no pillows, so they prop their heads on their rifles as they lay down between the knee-sized hills of trash that line the compound wall. Since the 2012 coup, Omar says, the trash still gets put out, but only occasionally taken away.

Omar's father, the owner, says nothing. He only appears in the early mornings, in the courtyard, where he silently eats a breakfast of sheep's liver and coffee. He will be gone by the time most of his guests wake up. Omar runs the place day to day, night to night.

That is, at least, how the hotel was when I visited. It was the third week of February 2013: Sony was announcing PlayStation 4, Oscar Pistorius had just popped Reeva Steenkamp, and A$AP Rocky's "Fuckin' Problems" topped the Billboard 100.

Some Qaedas, meanwhile, had spent the last year setting up a sprawling camp in north Mali, stockpiling Libyan ammo, and trafficking fighters to everywhere from Algeria to Nigeria and back again, with all routes leading back to that little trading outpost called Gao (population about 500,000).

No one much cared, until the French started to bomb them. And then, suddenly, everyone cared. It didn't last long — just a few weeks, between the last massacre in Syria and Egypt getting interesting again. But for that quick moment in history, every editor, analyst, jihad-junkie, and talk-show host in the West wanted to know what had been going on in a boondock desert town called Gao.

With the possible exception of the Steenkamp family's driveway, Gao was the single most relevant patch on Earth that week — the object of global contra-Qaeda obsession and the center of the geopolitical universe.

That's how it seemed to us, anyway. You have to remember: there was only one hotel.

I arrived on a Saturday night, after dark and after curfew, in a car with two other journalists: a fellow American newspaper writer, in her 50s and inexplicably clad in high-heeled boots and carrying no cash; and a thirtysomething freelance British cameraman obsessed with bullet taxonomy, my anatomy, and the journalist Anthony Loyd. Neither of them spoke French, so I translated at every checkpoint and roadside stall.

We'd started in Bamako a week earlier and headed north on the old highway, last paved by the French three generations ago, reaching the halfway point, Sevaré, eight hours and 400 miles later. From Sevaré onward, our Toyota Land Cruiser was tucked between two Nexter/Renault fighting vehicles, crawling at 30 miles per hour in a long French convoy sweeping for bombs. Sevaré was the furthest town north that the Qaedas hadn't reached. With the French now in-country, there was no going north of Sevaré without the military escort.

Occasionally we'd stop, for a few hours of bivouac sleep or for the French to tend to an overheated and broken-down tank. They fed us from their spare rations of rabbit terrine and goat's cheese, and the ones who'd previously served in Afghanistan informed me more than once that, "Your army eats like shit."

Past Douentza, past Dogon country, the streams of barefoot children waving tricolors began to thin. The beaming grandmothers disappeared from the doorways of their huts as the savannah became desert and the desert became badland. Blackened, mangled chunks of bombed-out Qaeda cars appeared on the sides of the road, like giant skeletons charring in the sun — the work of French missiles a few days earlier.

At the Gao city limits, the French wished us luck and peeled off for their base outside town. The sun had gone down and the streets were empty. We had no directions, no clue at all except that we were in Gao and that Gao had a hotel.

We drove and drove, past darkened houses and shuttered shops. Finally, we saw the matte glow of fluorescent light from behind a compound wall. "That's it," said the Brit. We had found the hotel.

We parked at the gate and dropped our bags in the courtyard. Tinny jazz guitar wafted through the cracked window of one of the rooms, accompanied by soft Francophone chatter and hash-laced plumes of cigarette smoke.

From the main building, dimly lit with the generator rumbling, Omar shuffled toward us. At a backlit distance, he appeared 50 at least, walking slow and hunched in a baggy gray *boubou*. As he came closer, I saw he was no older than 30, with a hard-cut jaw and a juvenile pout set on his lips.

He didn't greet his new arrivals, only eyed us each up and down. Then: "I have no rooms," he said, "and only one mattress left on the roof."

He spoke clean French, low and sighing as they do in the suburbs of Paris. Not the usual staccato stuff of francophone Africa. He had the air of an overgrown teenager, the same ambivalent lean of any man in any city who still lives with his parents past a certain age. He rubbed the stubble on his jaw, before adding: "Tomorrow."

"We'll sleep in the courtyard tonight and pay full," I replied. "Or on the roof without a mattress. We don't care."

Omar waited a beat. "You'll pay in full and in advance?"

We nodded and pulled wads of bills from our money-belts, while Omar made a huffing, sighing show of considering the matter. At last: "Wait here. I'll get you blankets."

The other American unloaded her tangle of electronics and went to hunch over the generator, which was already wheezing under a larger tangle of French electronics that had gotten there first. The Brit excused himself to go find "Johnny," a local bootlegger we'd heard about from some Belgians in Sevaré.

Johnny turned out to be just outside the hotel, around the corner from the gate, concluding some business with the night guard. He was not hard to spot, in a metallic turquoise *boubou* and long gold chains glinting moonlight. Slung over his shoulder was an ugly black leather bag, bulging with his wares: small plastic sacks from Ghana marked "gin" and "whiskey," desert weed consisting mainly of seeds and stems, hard blackish-brown lumps of hash, carved wooden statues and bead-and-metal jewelry, cocaine, tribal swords and knives, and anything else a visitor might require.

"I love this war," the Brit hissed to me, leaning against the courtyard wall to wait. "This is definitely my favorite war."

"Shut up," I hissed back. He'd been saying that for a week, all through the drive up. "Stop saying that."

I left the Brit and Johnny to their negotiations, and turned to follow the music inside the hotel and down the hall, where a French photographer was hosting a party. Olive-skinned TV presenters from Paris lounged on his bed, sleek in black fitted cargo pants and low-cut cotton, sipping gin and lemonade from teacups and flicking through the photographer's portfolio on an iPad. Their apple-shaped cameramen leaned against the walls, studying their frames from the day and passing a spliff between them. By the window, a German newswire stringer fought with a gin packet, ripping with his teeth until it split and spilled over the notebook in his shirt pocket.

The photographer stood when I entered and flicked a lock of white hair from his forehead.

He produced a pocket knife from his crisp blue jeans and sliced open a fresh sac of Johnny's gin. "Welcome to Gao, American girl." He poured the gin into a teacup, with ginger ale and a wedge of lime, and handed it to me, adding: "How do you like our little war?"

There was a hotel before all this.

The Qaedas had been building their Saharan network through Gao for years. After the coup in 2012, their lieutenants in the MUJAO franchise — the "Movement for Oneness and Jihad in West Africa" — began administering the town. They'd shuttered the bars and nightclubs and confiscated the cigarettes.

Anything else that the separatists hadn't ransacked, the Qaeda's MUJAO occupied and ran: the hospital, the prison, the roads, the market. Government buildings, prime real estate. A hotel. Every passer-through needs a place to sleep — quiet and secure, with *en-suite* plumbing and intermittent electricity. And for some time, Gao had been as quiet as it gets.

When Paris sent Rafale fighter jets screaming through the sky, Gao and its hotel lurched wide awake. The Qaedas fled to the mountains and the MUJAO went to the river. Men like Omar and his father, the neighbors gossiped, shaved their beards and put their Qaeda-approved cutoff pants back in the drawer. Uniformed soldiers replaced the men in black guarding the hotel.

By the third week of February, as I finally laid down in a cold corner of Omar's roof without a mattress, the whole world was watching Gao. But long before that, even when Gao had been silent and forgotten as a dead man's memory, there had been a hotel, and there had been guests.

Two days after I arrived, a handful of French and the high-heeled American set out for Timbuktu, and I was upgraded to my own room. From the barred window over my bed, I could see the rotisserie across the street. There, for about $5 you'll get a large sack of mutton, freshly slaughtered and barbecued, chopped to bits by a black crow of a man and shaken with onion and powdered red pepper.

This is an excellent breakfast, or lunch, or dinner. It's as much mutton as you'd ever want for $5. But you can't have the organs. I asked, but no: The liver, kidneys, and heart all go — the rotisserie man points — to Omar's father, to the old landlord across the street, who eats them for breakfast every morning.

Next door is a small convenience stall, which by that third week of February was already back in the business of selling cigarettes. There were two brands available: "Liberté Blonde" and "American Legend," both bearing dubious "Communauté Européenne" stamps on the packets. Being a blonde American, I always bought one of each. The stall also sells canned peas and carrots, to go with your mutton; candles, flip-flops, matches, toothbrushes — everything that is not worth Johnny's time.

From there it's a five-minute drive to the city center, the market and the main square, the town hall and the courthouse. I spent my first few days interviewing schoolteachers, utility workers, stall owners, a doctor. Everyone wanted to talk. There had been no one new to tell anything to for so long.

The most popular sights among the journalists then were the sacked and abandoned villas. These had been local officials' homes, once, in the tonier streets outside the center, which the officials had fled after the coup and which were promptly occupied by visiting Qaedas and their entourages. We pawed through the rubble of what the French had bombed and the Malians had raided. It was all interesting, or none of it was: documents, pharmaceuticals, ancient family snapshots and duplicate photographs for IDs from governments that no longer existed; spent ammunition and piles of records, rubbish and bullshit from strings of lives going back a decade or more.

Neighborhood kids usually joined in our pilfering, recounting stories of the previous tenants. "They beat us!" they chirped. "And we had to wear the scarf!" shrieked the girls. "If we didn't" — *THWACK* against a friend's arm, everyone dissolving into giggles — "They BEAT us!"

Nearby, their mothers smiled politely as they bent into the debris, scavenging bits of cloth and burnable wood.

The hotel is named after one of the old Songhai emperors. I won't tell you which.

There was, I'm sure, a hotel there even then, under some other name, back before the Moroccans invaded, when Gao had its quick century-and-a-half as the capital of one of the largest Islamic empires the world had ever known.

After a few days around town and more notes than I had electricity to type up, I got in the habit of staying late in the hotel. The French and the rest left early in the day to catch the morning light on their cameras. I took up my post at a table in the courtyard, where I smoked and mainlined Nescafé and pretended to write.

By nine, Omar left for the mosque and an errand or two, and his three servant girls emerged from the kitchen. None older than 16, they removed their headscarves and smirked at me as they carted teacups of gin and overflowing ashtrays from inside our rooms. Always, within a few minutes, the heaviest-set one would approach my table and jab a finger at my laptop, rolling her hips and grinning suggestively. She wanted me to produce music from the thing. She wanted to dance.

They spoke no French and I no Songhai. I'd mime back that I couldn't comply — *It's a shit machine*, I'd say, banging the back of the dented HP — *it's a workhorse, no good for fun and games and secret dance parties*. I'd stand up and we'd dance anyway, jerking our heads and jutting our hips to an imaginary rhythm. After a few minutes, I'd mime that I needed to resume working on my piece-a-crap no-fun machine. By the time Omar returned, the rooms were clean and the girls had disappeared back into the kitchen.

Omar wasn't much to talk to, at least not about Gao, not about the war, not about the Qaedas or the MUJAO or the Tuareg separatists, or anyone really. I asked him once if the servant girls were his wives. "They're sort of like family," he replied, by which the French guessed he meant slaves.

We all pressed him, on which groups had done what, where and how and to whom, but he was useless. Everyone had done everything, he said — the Qaedas and all the rest — and he had no idea what.

But we got along, Omar and me, mostly thanks to my steady supply of cigarettes and the fact that my meager electronics demanded so little of his generator.

And he talked about other things — anything but here-and-now — in the mornings when the courtyard was empty. He questioned my thoughts on rap, having once lived for Public Enemy and Dr. Dre, "when I was a kid. I was a bad kid." He expounded on the East Coast versus West Coast divides, and other esoteric matters within the subgenres. The music may be bad, *haram*, but he could still discuss its finer points.

He talked about the "old times," too — his own supposedly distant past. Turned out that before Omar became the heir and manager to the only hotel in Gao, with teenage servant girls holding secret parties in his absence and stoned gunmen at the gate, he had been, as he put it, of the "diplobrat" set. His father, the mute old man who eats sheep guts every morning, had once ranked high in the UN. The family had spent most of the 1990s moving through capitals across Africa.

After that, Omar's details haze out. The family came home, to Gao. Omar found God and became "good." His father retired from the UN. A new life started: the hotel, the other properties, and eventually the warring, the occupations, the piles of trash and the apoplectic generator, and the sense that Gao could disappear whole into the earth without anyone outside noticing or caring.

We joked about the French being pains in the ass. They'd been going through Omar's teacup supply three times over every night, and dropping cigarette butts down the toilet when their ashtrays were full. The Brit, Omar rolled his eyes, left his shoes and documents and cameras strewn across the courtyard. He and the German drank too much, too openly. And the other American, before she'd left for Timbuktu — "why do you people need so much water?" Omar demanded.

Still, Western media types weren't the worst guests Omar had had. "At least with the journalists here," he told me once with the curl of a smile, "I know there won't be any missiles landing in my courtyard."

On the fifth morning, that third week of February, I woke up to pounding. Lots of pounding. Something pounding in the distance, down the road toward the market, the sharp crack of gunpowder breaking stone. And someone pounding on my door.

First things first: "What?" I threw open my door.

It wasn't seven o'clock yet, but in the courtyard the Frenchies and the Brit and the German had already begun to assemble. Omar stood outside my door, stooped into a crescent and squinting through his glasses. "You're not going out, are you?"

"Where? What's happening?"

Behind him, the journalists were frantically picking their equipment wires from the flaps of their body armor. "The war's happening!" the Brit cried over Omar's shoulder. "Someone's just shredded the market. It's all happening downtown, it's big. We're leaving in 10 minutes, hurry up."

Omar, still at my door, stared at his feet and shook his head. "You shouldn't go. Nobody should go anywhere. Please. Stay here, do not leave the hotel."

A few minutes later, I was clipped into my own Kevlar vest and helmet, both oversized loans from a cameraman in Bamako, and bouncing in the back cab of a Malian army truck. We drove until we reached the courthouse, at the center of town. The truck emptied. I couldn't believe how loud the explosions were then. I still can't believe it.

I followed the Malian soldiers and a handful of French journalists to the side of the courthouse wall, where we crept to the edge of the compound. A motorcycle tore across the street, one swaddled MUJAO at the handlebars and another straddled off the back, spraying a Kalashnikov behind them in a 180-degree curve. It felt like a movie set. What made it most real was the pounding of my own heart, so violent against my thoracic cavity that I was sure it would explode and send shards of sternum into the street like shrapnel.

At the edge of the compound, we ducked and waited till the street was clear before running to the next wall of cement that wrapped the town hall. From the other side of the structures, we could hear the Malian army trying to storm the compound gates with Dushkas and Kalashnikovs, against MUJAO fighters holed up inside with grenades and bomb belts. Beyond that, shattering cracks ripped from the market stalls, booby-trapped the night before.

Inside my chest, striated myocytes lurched against convulsing pectoralis as I watched the others, one by one, dash across the dirt road to the relative safety of the next wall. I was the last to cross the street. I was halfway there when suddenly I was on the ground, my nose and mouth pressed into the dirt.

I knew I hadn't been shot. I'd stumbled on the rocks and lost my balance, the cameraman's heavy vest sliding off my shoulders and down toward the earth. I hadn't been shot. But for a quarter-second on the ground, I knew — or I thought I knew — that I was *about* to be shot. I was wrong, but I could see it as if it was happening: the motorcycle screaming down the road and that MUJAO slamming a bullet into my back, or hoisting me up by the hair and dragging me to a Qaeda-hostage house. I knew without a doubt that my mother was in for terrible news, and the worst part was remembering that I had been warned. Omar had been right. I should have stayed in the hotel.

The quarter-second ended eventually and my feet started moving. I got up from the ground and crossed the street to the cover of the cement wall, the Kevlar vest swinging like a bag of rocks across me and my helmet down over my eyes.

I made it back to the hotel by mid-afternoon. A few of the French had already returned, but they hadn't given Omar much news before heading to the roof to transmit their dispatches. I told Omar what I'd seen and heard, though the battle had already begun to tumble and compress in my skull. I told him I couldn't believe how loud the grenades and Kalashnikovs had been, and the bombs cracking through the marketplace, and how by the time the French soldiers finally arrived and a carload of TV crewsters scooped me up and drove me away, a bulbous plume of black smoke was rising from the flaming gas station next to the marketplace, curling high into the bluest sky.

Omar removed his glasses as he listened and rubbed his face so hard it looked like he might peel off his eyelids. Eventually he said: "I didn't think they would do this."

I drained a lukewarm bottle of water someone had left in a corner of the courtyard.

"Well," I replied, then didn't say: *They did.*

I went to my room to work and wash. When I was done, the rest of the journalists were back and assembling in the courtyard. Their eyes were glazed and their faces draped in dumb grins that probably matched mine, which simply said *You're alive? I'm alive!*

With his guests safely returned, Omar vanished for the night. The journalists stayed up late and drank. The rotisserie stall had shuttered for the day, so dinner consisted of power bars and hoarded French rations from the drive up. We drained our Johnny-supplies as the cameramen compared footage, playing and replaying the scenes of Gao's wreckage, now digitized forever and bound for millions of eyeballs around the world.

"This is the best war ever," the Brit intoned when his laptop battery finally died. I asked him to shut up, but he ignored me. "*C'est ma guerre préférée.*"

I was back on the road to Bamako two days later, as soon as the French reopened the main artery out of town. Omar was still asleep when my car pulled away, but I'd paid in advance. I nodded to the soldiers, and at the old man staring straight ahead over his breakfast of sheep guts. The three servant girls loaded my bags into the car. I handed them cash and mimed that I'd be back soon — the obligatory lie. They laughed and waved my Land Cruiser down the road.

That was a long time ago now, and getting longer. I scan the news for word from Gao, though there isn't much and what there is isn't good. The world forgot about Gao again very quickly after that February. Most of the French are gone, their soldiers and their press. The Brit and the German have both gone to Syria, where the Islamic statists have overshadowed the Qaedas for some time. Mali recently had a round of headlines in the press, when Qaedas took 170 hostages and killed 20 at a Radisson in the capital.

By all appearances, plenty of Qaedas remain in Gao, along with a few thousand UN blue-helmets. Who occupies Omar's courtyard these days, or what flags drape the trucks of the armed gunmen at his gate, I can't imagine. But I assume Omar is still there, with all his fucking problems, and his old father too. The servant girls may have moved on, and I work hard not to wonder where or what to.

There is still a hotel. That much, I guarantee. You'll find it if you go, and while I don't advise that you do, I can't recommend the hotel highly enough. A room for the night, quiet and secure, with *en-suite* plumbing and intermittent electricity. It's all there, I promise. As long as Gao remains a place at all, there will be a hotel — for me, for the Qaedas, and for any other stranger who might pass through.

Friends in LA MIKE DAVIS

IN THE FIRST LA I have friends who would nonchalantly sip lattes without adjusting their sunglasses as they sidestepped my pitiful corpse.

In the second LA I have friends who seeing me dead would immediately wonder where they could publish the obituary but regret that I'm not alive to provide a blurb for their new book.

In the third LA I have old partners in crime who'd lie in the grave next to me as long as we died for the kids.

....

In the first LA they say, "Love you dude, you're awesome. Give me five, and let's touch base soon." Sure.

In the second LA people ask, "Have you read my manuscript" — they always seem on the verge of a heart attack.

In the third LA, comrades debate "What is to be done?" and share cheap wine in a paper bag.

(You a dog, Ron, but the Third Man, you.)

< FAY RAY
TWO RINGS, 2015
COATED MYLAR, ALUMINUM, GALVANIZED WIRE ROPE
PHOTOGRAPHY BY JOSHUA WHITE/JWPICTURES.COM

Postcard HELEN MALMGREN

OH JUST LOOK AT THEM. White sock and black sock. Big brother and kid brother. Joker and Butt of the Joke. What do you think Joker is dropping down the back of Butt's sweater, even as they pose for the photo?

Photographs of siblings always tell you the real story of the family. They can't help it — they're all fighting for first place all the time. They can't just turn it off for a Christmas card picture.

The most telling photo of my father's family is a picture of two brothers — my father, Tom, and his twin brother, Jerry. (Yes, I know. That was a mistake. My grandparents wrote "Thomas" and "Jerald" on the birth certificates, and didn't realize what they'd done until it was too late.) Anyway, in the photo that I'm thinking of, my father is just home from the war in Korea. He's gorgeous, with a big wool coat, military cap, sharp haircut, confident eyes.

He'd run away from home at age 15, changed his birth certificate, and joined the Air Force, three years before he was old enough to do so legally. And he'd pulled it off! And he'd come back a man!

His parents took that photo of him, and hung it on the wall.

It was years before I realized that my uncle Jerry, whom I later knew as my drunk Uncle Jerry, was also in the photo. There he is, barely visible in the background.

"Where was he when you were in Korea?" I asked my dad when I finally noticed Jerry in the photo.

"Oh, Jerry was in Korea too," he said. "He ran away and enlisted a week after I did. He just didn't make it into the picture."

To a Story

DAVID ST. JOHN

We'd become friends after I rented the empty studio
          behind her redwood house in Tiburon

As soon as she asked if I was good with my hands
          I understood she had a few things

That might need fixing around the place including
          her Jag convertible an old '54 XK120

Aged to a dull bullet-silver by the salty Bay air
          the walnut dash framing those twin

Disks of its black gauges   speedometer & tach
          & you know there's nothing I love

Like an elegant restoration in loving progress
          – stop giving me that look –

Her ex-husband Edison had even left a few berets
          in the closet hung above his oil paints

& I loved that old studio its raw uneven redwood
          planks letting in the soft fog at night

As well as those delicate early Brahms sonatas
          she'd practice as her ritual before

Leaving on tour & then always away a month or more
          so I'd watch the place & bring in the mail

& guard her koi pond from skinny dog-sized raccoons
          cruising up the narrow lanes at night

One morning she called out of the blue on her layover
in Reykjavik & just started screaming

How *Esquire* had a story in it about her – not one of
those devoted profiles she knew well

But a piece of actual fiction – *A story about her! by Edison*
& she hated him truly

After letting him get away with endless affairs & years
of good drugs & bad rehab she'd paid for

– & finally he'd gone too far   he'd made her into
nothing but a story & worse claimed

She'd been older than she was when they first met
& now she was screaming so loudly

I'm pretty sure most of Iceland could hear her say
That fucking bastard even made me

Throw out the black panties Keith Richards signed for me
& I said Ilaria!   just focus! –

Everybody knows Edison's a liar!   & then a long
silence exquisitely cold as Reykjavik

Before I heard   *I am going now to catch my plane*
more silence & then   *Don't leave me* ⁄⁄

CITY NIGHTMARES

HISHAM BUSTANI
TRANSLATED BY MAIA TABET

[*The building that sees, hears, and speaks*]

The building is dark and gloomy, full of ghosts from the past. They wander around, in and out of apartments and rooms, and up and down the stairwell. Like people, the building can see and hear, and it can also speak: its eyes stare out of the windows and from the cracks in the walls; it listens through the downspouts of the rain gutters and from the bathroom windows that open onto the ventilation shaft; and it speaks ... oh, how it speaks.

"Bitch!" "Bastard!" I could hear my uncle and his wife scream on the second floor, their endless disagreements, like an old broken record. Then came the sound of shattering glass and slamming doors, and the building shuddered like an old refrigerator.

I was always alone. Every day, I'd sit on the stairs outside, as if I were waiting. I waited for a bus to take me far away, but the bus never came. Once, I envisioned it falling from the sky, but it was just a tile that had fallen so close it brushed up against my scent before crashing to the ground and breaking. I recoiled like a loaded spring and looked up: there was no one up there, and the roof wasn't even tiled. I would remember that later, when tiles rained down from the sky.

They were hitting each other. My uncle was up to his ears in debt, and his wife was expected to keep up appearances. But the wall cracked, the nail was dislodged, and the picture shattered ... frame, glass, and all. Tiptoeing past her slumber-filled eyes, Uncle fled his wife, his creditors, and everyone he knew. He went to Cairo and died there.

That morning, you could hear a mother beating her children, and when she came out of the building, her purse in hand, I was still sitting on the stairs in front, waiting for the bus.

To top it all off — the children's wailing and the mayhem — she spat on me.

[*The bus that never comes*]

It is green as green pastures, the doors don't close, the windows are glassless, and the seats are made of Damask roses. Its passengers are all friends of mine: Dante, Stendhal, Yann Tiersen, Mourid Barghouti ... oh, and it is full of cats, and birds too. Driverless, it runs on wheels made of music, and there is no conductor.

At every stop, they all disembark, spread out a rug, and sit around with glasses of wine and wedges of cheese, as well as garlic *labaneh* and seeded whole-wheat bread. They keep a trash bag close. The soldiers toss in their rifles and boots, the informer his eyes and ears, the bougie lady her high heels, the pupil his teacher, the opportunist his position, the prostitute her society, and the Almighty Leader his very self.

Only then do they all raise a toast to love and freedom. They bare themselves, detail their failings, their traumas, and their hang-ups, and become one copulating body in a grand orgy before scattering back to their separate selves, climbing hand in hand aboard the bus, and going on to the next stop.

But the bus never comes.

[*The Ghost Room*]

Oh, my, how that building spoke …

My widowed grandmother lived on the ground floor. She'd lost her husband before I was born, and had stayed on in the building even after all the other residents had left.

"I made friends with the imprint of their fingerprints on the wall plates and with their dust bunnies under the armchairs. If I leave, I won't have anything left of them. Like this, at least their ghosts remain."

"Here is where my first child fell and bled, and here, on top of this wardrobe, is where your father hid from his father after he'd broken the window and caught sight of the black belt in the furious fist bent on finding him."

She would skirt around the corners and the pieces of furniture and tell stories. The second floor brought on a torrent of tears. "I will never see him again." That's what she said when he stole away to Cairo, and when he died there. Only one room at the far end of her apartment remained closed. She never spoke about it or let me go near it.

Sometimes, I managed to give her the slip and would go and glue myself to the keyhole. I could barely make out the sound of a labored and pained voice, but no words.

One day, when I couldn't stand waiting for the bus anymore and my stomach was growling, I went to find her, but no one was on the ground floor. "Nana, Grandma," I called, wondering where a barely ambulant old woman could go, and how she could have passed me — I'd been at the door of the building since morning.

The house was spotless, its floors and walls gleaming. No dirty fingerprints on the electric switch plates and no dust bunnies under the armchairs. Everything looked spanking new, as if it had been wrapped and the wrapping had just been taken off. And the door to the forbidden room lay open.

I approached, tiptoeing, and was startled by the darkness and the deep and wordless moans. As my eyes grew accustomed to the dark, my grandfather appeared, sitting by the bed like the arches of an ancient aqueduct, bent over double, his head propped in his hands, his fingers squeezing his eyes as he suppressed a feverish sob. On the bed lay a small, immobile, black figure: a charred and desiccated me.

With memories of mouse rooms, ghost rooms, as well as the dark under-the-stair closets and their accumulated terror, I darted out of the room, running from the apartment and out through the door of the building onto the street.

[*A fleeting visit to what once was*]

I ran out of the room, out of the apartment, out of the building door and onto the street, panting, my pulse pounding like the drums of war, throbbing through the veins of my hands, my ears, my temples, feeling as if I was going to explode. For a second, I pulled myself together and looked behind me — there I was all in black, standing at the door of the building. As soon as my eyes met my eyes, I ran behind myself, and almost fell. Night descended suddenly, and I slammed into a high wall.

"It's the end of the road," shouted a gravelly voice.

I turned around and found that I was face to face with myself. Adrenaline rushing, pupils fully dilated, I began to shake: silent as a stone, immobile as a wall overgrown with vines, features erased and tinted lemon yellow.

I was struggling to open my eyes, desperate to wake up, but it felt as if invisible fingers were holding them tightly shut. I managed to pull together every bit of strength I had left. I transformed it into a chisel and a hammer, which I banged so hard that my eyelids opened. Aaahhhh, I gasped, sucking all the air out of the room. I burst into tears and began sobbing.

I felt so sleepy. I was dead tired but didn't want to go back to that room, on that street with the wall blocking it, to that other me, and the feeling that I couldn't open my eyes. I was shaking like a leaf.

She heard children's voices far away. She brushed away her tears and looked out of the window. There were four of them, coming out of their school overlooking the Qal'aa near the *hawuz* on Jabal al-Lweibdeh, wearing shorts made by capable mothers who passed them down from sibling to sibling. The sign read: "School of Islamic Sciences — founder Tayseer Dhibian." This is now 1946.

The children trotted down the dirt road toward the Tash orchard, and when they reached the stone enclosure, they jumped the wall. They filled their empty little bellies with green almonds or figs — filling their pockets while they were at it as the day was still long. They crossed over to the other side of the orchard, leaped over the wall again and out onto an open space that overlooked Wadi Saqra, with Jabal Amman rising behind it. In the little clearing, they lined up their stones and split into two teams. She heard them crying out *gird-ou-sharah*. She didn't know that game.

Once they were done playing, they sat on the edge of the bluff, looking into the distance at the Circassians' ox-drawn carts making their way up the dirt road that traversed the orchards and wound around to Wadi al-Seer all the way from the city center. They got back up to play, standing on the rocks and boulders, rolling those they could dislodge from the top of the hill down into the bowl of the valley, uncovering a spider, snake, or lizard. Lizards had pride of place among the reptiles: painted on the palms of the children's hands, their blood was a palliative to the teacher's rod.

As the sun began its descent on the horizon, the children went looking for nature's candy — the *furqo'* they delighted in eating. By the time the sun had gone down behind the mountains, they had gathered mallow, dandelion, and hawkweed, wild greens they would have for dinner — their mothers' injunctions would not be ignored.

When they got back to the *hawuz*, and before each boy went his way, the four of them turned toward her and waved goodbye as they melted into the gathering darkness.

She closed her window and peacefully dissolved into a deep sleep.

[*When Tiles Rained Down from the Sky*]

I was still sitting in front of the building door, stark naked and waiting for the bus, with nothing to toss into the trash bag before climbing aboard, when the sky darkened. The clouds were unlike any I had ever seen before: white and steely, so low you could see their particles, and it made you want to sneeze … their thunder an endless crashing of sheet metal.

It was only seconds before the first drop fell: a tile that shattered beside me on the ground. "But the roof isn't tiled," I thought to myself. Before I could finish the sentence, down came another, then a third, and a fourth … then a torrent of tiles, cut stone, window glass, and flying pieces of furniture.

I ran to get away from the downpour, crossed the street, and jumped onto the neighbors' balcony. I looked across the way: lifting off the ground was a thick gray fog smothering everything.

As the cloud dispersed, a yellow monster with metal jaws and big elliptical rubber feet sat atop the building, or what was left of it.

He winked at me from the glass eye at the center of his small head, raucously belching out a plume of smoke. The sky was overcast again with the same kind of clouds I had just seen for the first time … and that same metallic crash of thunder.

[*Downtown*]

Welcome! Welcome to Abdali!

Gaping holes in the ground and narrow metal cranes rotating on their axes hoisting concrete slabs and stacks of breeze blocks and steel.

Welcome to what is slated to become Amman's new downtown. Amman has no old downtown for it to have a new one. Amman used to have a city center. But now, in the era of big-box stores and packaged things, Amman is to acquire a downtown, possibly even a Centre Ville, like Beirut's. The umbilical cord between them is the same: Solidère Beirut and Solidère Amman are one. The same Hariri silken glove destroying and "developing" in order to line the same pockets with billion-dollar profits — the difference only in whose pockets are being lined, and the cuts and contracts that ensue.

Welcome, welcome to Abdali!

All along the periphery of majestic Jabal al-Lweibdeh, bulldozers had set to work. The project was extended even before the land had been expropriated. It was all planned in advance, like an act of God, an inescapable stroke of fate.

Amman's mischievous children used to roll boulders and rocks from Jabal al-Lweibdeh to the bottom of Wadi Saqra, dislodging the snakes, spiders, and lizards underneath (at a time now long gone). Whenever they found a new friend under one of the rocks, they squealed with delight, their little feet scurrying to chase after it.

Today, it is rocks and concrete slabs that hurl people down from the mountaintop — with memories, histories, and photos shattering in the plain below. And no sooner are the old houses brought down than everything below is pulverized by a colossal footstep, leaving in its wake a crater dozens of meters deep.

Welcome, welcome to Amman's new downtown.

Behind the huge full-color banners ringing the area with images of a delusional future, there's nothing but dust, excavation sites, and cranes — and workers trucked in from faraway places whose sweat is wrung dry with impunity.

A blistering sun beats down on the leveled land, now devoid of trees, of people, and of memories; enveloped in rays of gold, a lovely young woman runs, terrified and directionless, as though pursued. She stops suddenly. "The building was here," she says, then starts running again. She stops once more. "No, it was here." She runs and runs and runs. The building was here … no, here … or rather, here.

Soon, someone is pursuing her: a security detail in charge of guarding the project. What does she want, they ask, catching up with her. What is she looking for?

"For the bus stop where the bus never comes," she replies, out of breath.

NOTES

Hawuz is a water tower or reservoir, usually erected on the highest point of an elevation to use gravity and thus facilitate the flow of water.

The **four friends** were Abdel-Hadi Shuqayr, Abdel-Fattah al-Bustani, Mohammad Khamis, and, his brother, Shafiq Khamis.

The **Tash orchard** on Jabal al-Lweibdeh was a grove of fruit trees that belonged to Mohammad Tash. It was eventually razed and its green expanse covered with residential buildings.

Gird-ou-sharah, Monkey and Emblem, was a popular game among Amman's children.

Furqo' is an edible wild tuber that looks and tastes like a chestnut. While it grows underground, its foliage boasts cascading white flowers.

Jabal al-Lweibdeh, ***Jabal Amman***, and ***Jabal al-Qal'aa*** are three of the seven hills on which modern Amman was established. In Arabic, *jabal* is a mountain and *wadi* is a valley, hence ***Wadi Saqra*** and ***Wadi al-Seer*** are two of the valleys between the hills. ***Al-Qal'aa***, the citadel, is a walled site atop one of the seven hills, which dates back to the Bronze Age. It is dotted with the remains of Byzantine, Roman, and Umayyad buildings, including an Umayyad palace, a temple dedicated to Hercules, and a Byzantine church.

Solidère is the real estate development company that took over Beirut's war-ravaged downtown after the end of the Lebanese Civil War (1975–'91).

[*Discarded Photo Album*]
An Indian laborer found these photos in a torn-up album in the rubble of the (demolished) building. They were placed in safekeeping at the Archaeological Museum in Jabal al-Qal'aa. The captions, written in blue ink on the back of the photos, are reproduced below.

Mohammad Khamis (first row, first from right); Shafiq Khamis (first row, second from right); Abdel-Fattah al-Bustani (first row, second from left); Abdel-Hadi Shuqayr (first row, third from left), with Akram al-Khatib, their teacher (center), in front of the School of Islamic Sciences.

The School of Islamic Sciences scout troop, including the four friends. The school building is visible to the left.

A visit by the venerable Sheikh Tayyib al-Aqabi al-Jaza'iri to the School of Islamic Sciences. To his right is Sheikh Nadeem al-Mallah, and in the back, on the top right, and wearing a tarboosh (fez), is the school's founder, Tayseer Dhibian.

Left: *Abdel Hadi Shuqayr (R), Abdel-Fattah al-Bustani (L), friends.*
Right: *Abdel-Fattah al-Bustani in front of the* hawuz *on Jabal al-Lweibdeh.*

GORING BEAUTY

COLIN DAYAN

I TRY TO ARRANGE the photographs. They were developed by my father sometime after he returned from his honeymoon in Mexico. I do not know what to call the man in the embroidered costume; he looks vaguely Spanish. He is a killer, but a killer with a flourish. He spins round the bull and spears it, looking down so gravely at the stricken animal. No, the spear or sword or lance is already in the shoulder, broken in two, over the raised wreck of flesh. So what is he doing? In one photo he holds a cape. It must be red. Isn't that the story I heard? "Bulls don't like red," my father told me. So one flash of a cape, and the bull "goes mad."

A pile of 24 black-and-white photos lie on my desk. I recognize the same man in 13 of them. I know him by the waves in his hair. Is he a matador? Or is it the picador? The one who stabs and pierces flesh. My father. Sweet Edmond. Kind Edmond. The bull's legs catch my attention. Holding tight under the shock of a strike, the legs paw the earth, digging up the dust, kicking back in a stretch too graceful for the vile if choreographed assault. The great glory of man, dressed up and ready to harm. The head of the bull turns and dips toward the earth, as one front leg seems to find balance. All I have is the dizzying perception of legs spread and angled, holding on, digging down. The face of the man fades into the black thick pelt of the bull. I search now for expression in the eyes of the animal so assailed by the vain spectacle set to the prance of the killer. All I want is to catch some sense of the bull's feeling, sufficient in attentiveness — the will caught in photo after photo, until the end when the body falls to earth, stilled in the shadow of the man who struts and looks out at his admirers.

When my father and mother married in 1939, they moved from New York to Nashville, and then left for Mexico. They drove their Buick Super 8 from Guadalajara to Cuernavaca, traveling along roads Graham Greene first captured in *The Lawless Roads* and then in *The Power and the Glory*, but I doubt they ever read him. My father didn't like Catholics. I do not know any details of their journey. No one even told me stories. All that remains of the visit are hundreds of photographs. There was never any need for words.

Over 50 years later, more than half a century, I look at the pictures. Out of boxes and other wooden and steel containers, and buried deep under other albums, come these relics of a honeymoon.

Those days were not remembered. They were not part of anything I knew, nor did they make up any kind of beauty my parents might retrieve about a past when they might have known love or passion. I spent my life not knowing the difference between the two. There was no warmth in my house, no sight of a kiss, except once or twice when my father tried to peck at my mother's lips as if he was ashamed, a moment in time preserved for me now only in her grimace. Lust I knew. The long afternoon phone calls when my mother rested on her bed behind a door that was not quite shut. Her legs I could not see. They were under the sheet. I remember a hand moving quickly. Yes, between her legs. Yes, as she laughed and sounded different than usual. Or was that love, as one hand languidly moved up and down, and the other held the phone very close to the ear.

But now before me, there now on my desk, I try to get through my father's cracked leather-bound albums. A gift, a glorious preservation of a past otherwise lost forever. These photographs from the first months of their marriage lie in wait for me. Once I look at them I might know something beautiful that I did not know before.

My mother's face, caught in poses that were never off-guard or random, does not speak to me. She still has that immaculate quality of being purified of anything living. In one photo, bent down, stooping in the dirt and surrounded by parrots, she seems dead, her smile frozen for the camera. A bracelet on her arm and a tan on her flesh, dressed in white and hair pulled back, she looks down at the birds. But she is not really seeing.

Then there is the pose of glamour. Looking out at my father. Maybe she saw this fashion somewhere in some movie of the '30s, the hand drawn up on one side, sultry on the hip.

A beauty.

Some of the photographs are laid out 10 to a page, on black hard paper; the pictures one upon the other are taped down. To look through them I must lift each one separately. I can only see one at a time, at any time.

My mother never looked at the photos. She had no interest in revisiting the past. I did.

Once I moved to Nashville, the past began to fill the emptiness of my life. It came forward when I least expected it.

I look at the pictures of her, lifting them up out of boxes as though they were dirty. It felt the same as when I went through my mother's bedroom dresser drawers, fingering the bras and panties, pulling them up to find pictures of naked bodies, men in poses with a penis in hand, or a tongue on the buttocks.

But the bulls are different.

The bullfights are on large 8x10 prints. Taunted, prodded, stabbed, the animals know what it is to be killed by humans. They sense that something distinctly upbeat comes along with their suffering. They hear the glee in the shouts from the stands. What, I wonder, along with the bulls, causes such elation? It seems that the more stricken the animal, the louder come the euphoric shouts. In the photos, the people are white. Whatever their nationality, their skin is white. Some of the men smile. Others look entranced by the bull's persecution. They all wear suits. And what about the women? I look at their faces. Two women smile next to each other. Are they getting ready to laugh? Another breaks into a wide grin. Some look bored. One smirks. Another turns to her friend. Is she looking away from the dying bull, or sharing a joke? None look amazed or troubled. If I look through these photographs long enough, I begin to lose interest in the audience. Then, I look back at the bull. There.

I find something that pulls me into concern, a regard that will not quit. Not something so broad as torment — the horrific wariness, then involuntary capitulation of the bull as a general body of flesh moving steadily toward ruin — but instead things that touch my heart more strongly than I could have anticipated: the spin of a tail in a semicircle; the slight lifting up of a head, then a mouth shut tight or faintly open, the tongue unseen; a head bowed as the legs become straight, poised while preparing to stand precisely in the site of pain. I try to look at the eyes. The black of the bull is so deep that it is difficult to see something as definite as expression. Most of the photos were taken to get the conventional shape of the conflict, the black mass of bull and the costumed curves of man. But in a few, I can see brightness, an indecipherable touch of light, a bull's-eye view of the dismal panorama of cape flung out, the tormentor's feet rising from the ground as the dirt flies up into the eyes I had just begun to rely upon as something not marked by death. I feel now that each picture confirms suffering that is effectively without end.

The marriage was doomed. My father went to the bullfights. During those afternoons, what did my mother do? The man rides the horse, a carnival picador dressed as if for a state fair in Georgia, spearing the bull. The bull is real. The bull is too gorgeous to be killed. More beautiful than my mother, or at least alive to the touch in a way she could never be. As I remember my mother and her broken life, I can't stop thinking about the bulls, the many bulls isolated from their kind, released into spectacle, performing their agony, the light in their eyes slowly turning into dark.

Dust, photographs, pile upon pile. It hurt me to look at them. So I took all the photos, hundreds of them in albums, cases, loose, or whatever — and put them back in the garage. But I kept the bulls dying in effigy on my desk.

This is a story about how bulls die, the blood, the curve of horns, and the lift of a head in response to the matador's formal low passes. The bull's head is raised high as the body collapses. But the legs are strong in their denial, the poise still fierce even as the legs stand apart. Some writers suggest a shared physical delight between human and bull. I do not see that reciprocity here. It is an invention by humans, for humans.

In *On Bullfighting*, A. L. Kennedy describes the "curious, intense dance between two species [...] as blood wells out of the bull's wounds." But what kind of sharing could be had in such an encounter, and why do writers so often recall it as rare evidence of the reciprocity between species? The progression of the *corrida* from mutual alertness to the matador's deliberate stalking and the bull's growing exhaustion signals a peculiarly human cruelty. Terrible and majestic, yes, but also

absurd: self-importance masked by the stiff brio that comes across as play. “It is up to the bullfighter to make the bull play and to enforce the rules,” Hemingway reminds his readers in *Death in the Afternoon*. Then he adds, in a sleight of hand that gives his writing assurance at the very moment when it falters in glaring abstraction: “The bull has no desire to play, only to kill.” I look at the photo, with the bull’s back torn by the *pica*. Not a spear, exactly, and not a sword either, but a pick, a narrow wooden shaft with a steel point. Broken, the stick splinters in two.

I have no choice now but to look through the series of photographs that portray the matador — at least two different men in more than one fight, one with a ponytail and the other with a short coif, both in embroidered jackets — and the bull in the final passes of the cape, the still small step of the bull, a final surge, a momentary charge that is disrupted by the body that now seems heavy as lead, in places already caving in, soon to collapse, wounded, head lowered in a gentle arc, flanks heaving, tendons and muscles strained, legs bent with the shadow of his scrotum caught in one of the pictures, the end of the tail spinning so fast that the hair-become-feathers catches hold of my attention. Many times I look away. My mind drifts somewhere else, wondering why I no longer care about a honeymoon that left my mother cold, my father clueless. But not for long, since I am drawn again, brought to focus by the bull’s legs. They tell me all I need to know about phenomenal grace and something more than beauty, for how can feet fixed in dirt, then raised up in the air at the strike, muscled with life then holding on in death, a head swerved gently, perhaps nodding in recognition of hurt, be anything but compelling, more absorbing than the flourish of the man with the cape? I place all my hope in the fleshly pads of the underside of the bull’s hooves, in the head hanging weighty and too low, in the tail that never ceases to move soundlessly through the air, in one back leg pushed out straight either to move the bull forward or to keep the body still as the head turns massively into the cape. This cape is doubled over a wooden stick or rod. It is called the *muleta*. When the *muleta* appears, everyone knows this marks the third and final stage of the bullfight, when the bull is weary or *aplomado*: in Hemingway’s words, “he has been made heavy, he is like lead; he has usually lost his wind, and while his strength is still intact, his speed is gone.” Now the sword will be used.

Death by cape and by sword: in one picture, a sword and cape held out in one hand; in the next, the sword in the right hand, the cape in the other.

I have tried to put them in order, these photographs that stay on my desk. Thousands of negatives remain in the brown boxes in the garage. Perhaps they contain images my father chose not to develop in his darkroom so late at night when my mother had already turned her back on him.

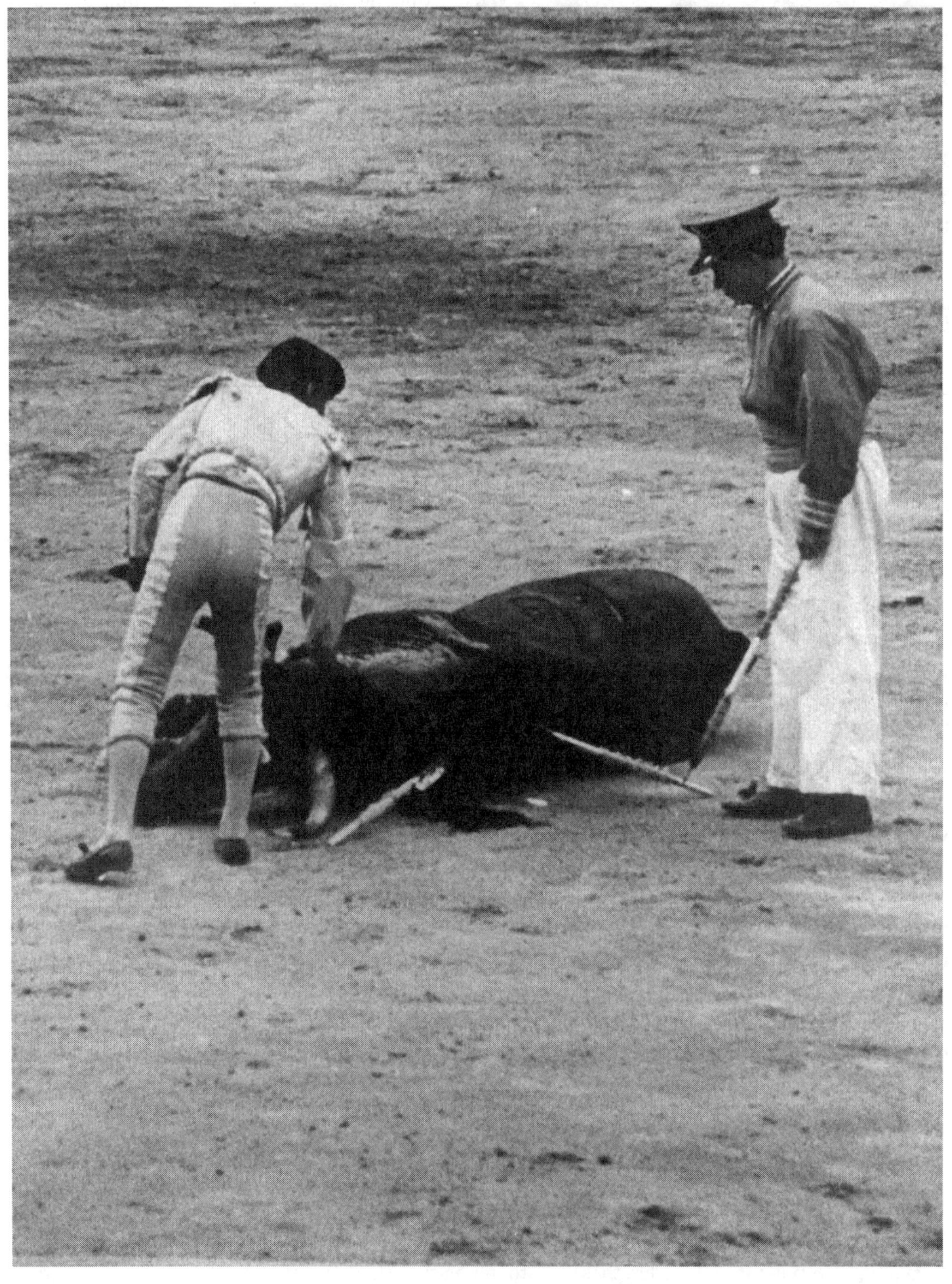

During the time I spent looking through the pile of photos, arranging them in some order that might make sense of them, a growing unease took hold of me. I stopped writing. Now when I go back to the desk I face pieces of a performance that no longer hold together, that cannot be made whole. I read again descriptions of the bullfight, as it should be or was, the ritual in three parts, with only one correct way of killing the bull, of rousing the crowds that watch it charge and die, of exhibiting the splendor and exact formality of the matador, with all his macabre grace.

Again I take the photographs and spread them out, all of them. Here is the picador in this single photo of a man on horseback, all a-jingle with his short jacket and tight breeches, like any other bullfighter except for the crazy white hat that sits on his head. And then there is the horse. Is he blindfolded? Horses die, and no one seems to mind. Even Hemingway admits the horror of such a death, entrails falling away from the wound — though he can't resist identifying disemboweling as one of those "strange and burlesque visceral accidents" so integral to the experience of the bullfight. There are no *banderilleros* or flagmen in sight, not in any of these photos. I see quite clearly the bull pelt made jagged, the flash of metal against the dazzling sun. Into that part of the neck atop the shoulders where muscles ripple comes the goad: as the bull tosses his head, these men plant barbed sticks that pierce the skin. Splendidly colored flags, paper strips, even ribbons are attached to these stick-blades, making a mockery of torment. Under this flutter of color and after many tiny stabs, the hump — the place between the neck and the top of the shoulder — is weakened, the muscles relaxed, the head lowered so that the sword can go in for the kill.

Now the bull collapses. Wearily, he sinks to the ground, resting it seems on one horn. The sound the sound the sound, I repeat to myself; what is the noise heard when the bull knows he is being murdered, when, deadly tired and pierced to the bone with picks, darts, and the ultimate lance thrust, he cries out in the arena to the cheers of a crowd? Who has written about the noise a bull makes? No one cares about the death rattles and groans, the bellowing that shakes up the performance with a strength that will not suffer humiliation.

The bull is dead in the sand, so huge and lost that he reminds me of a harpooned whale that has been washed to shore.

—

"Toro, toro," I hear the words in my mind. That nearly imperceptible memory comes to me now. I recall how we used to play bullfighter in my backyard. The game consisted of someone flashing a red scarf, or maybe a sheet of any color, in my face as I ran toward it. That was all: the lift of a cloth and my mad dash through it and beyond into some place where I lay along the dark earth in dead silence.

There I remained, hidden, my mouth open. I did not want to be the bull anymore.

ARTIST PORTFOLIO

ALEXIS SMITH

AMY GERSTLER

ALEXIS SMITH: She's sly as a coyote, and sharp as a sushi chef's favorite knife. Her wit's as dry as a completely vermouth-free martini. She's an image-text alchemist, a subtle, funny feminist, and a canny cultural critic, commenting on, and sometimes satirizing, truisms, collective identities, and what it means to be American.

Her art practice spans, at this point, almost 50 years. She cut her teeth during the 1970s, an era when the art world (if you can imagine this!) was even more of a boys' club than it is today. Alexis Smith is a master collagist and an inventive installation artist, as well as an architectural whiz with large public art projects in various American cities to her credit.

An early adopter of the practice of transforming cultural detritus into art, Smith has for decades haunted garage sales, thrift stores, and swap meets in search of materials. She's never shied away from a quick half gainer into a trash can to rescue cast offs that, when assembled into her work, tell tales of hubris, self-mythologizing, stereotyping, wanderlust (and just plain old carnal lust), and sometimes of politics skidding off the rails. Billboards, dime store novel covers, street signs, thrift store paintings, cigarettes, bullet casings, magazine pages, swizzle sticks, matchbooks, coasters, palm reader pamphlets, plastic toys, movie posters, play money, business cards, Ouija boards, cookie fortunes, fruit crate labels, trophy antlers, Girl Scout badges, prize ribbons, advertisements, astro turf ... all find new life and meaning in her work.

The various studios Smith has labored in over the decades, including her current workspace, are cabinets of curiosities, strange museums packed with her "finds," which are organized in drawers and plastic storage bins, or leaning against walls. Half-assembled collages are laid out on every available surface: tables, floor, chairs.

The first time I visited her, in her former studio in Venice, California, I was admitted to a storefront on Lincoln Boulevard, next door to a liquor store. "R. TIST" was the name discretely lettered in black onto one corner of the large frosted front window, a bit of wordplay typical of Smith. A bashed-in old upright piano, a dented tuba, a coffee shop sign, several signs from drive-in ice cream establishments and beauty shops were all in residence, as well as a collection of poignant, dinged up children's chairs, arranged in neat rows on a braided rug. It looked like a kindergarten, set up for child-ghosts.

Smith has a genius for seeing deeply, almost clairvoyantly, into the lives of objects. She brings their two- and three-dimensional selves into rich relation with each other, often including bits of text. From these ingredients she creates a new, eloquent, wry, succinct entity, in her page- or mural- or room- or building-sized collages.

She's fascinated by juxtaposition, by metaphor, by the relationship between words and pictures and things, by the ways she can combine them to hum and buzz and croon or clash and moan together, in the different layered languages spoken by objects and words, trailing their tangled mantles of connotation and denotation. She's entranced by what she calls "the associative power of images," by the way they can become emblematic of myths America and Americans generate about themselves. Alexis Smith's work covertly proposes that perhaps a poetic corrective is needed to offset the pitfalls of taking those fables too much to heart.

Joseph Cornell's sensibility is much akin to Smith's, though Cornell's taste was more delicate and Victorian, whereas Smith takes as her material the sometimes slightly grungy flotsam and jetsam of the popular culture of her childhood, and beyond. In a time when the vexed notion of "The American Dream" is expanding, contracting, and undergoing much needed challenge and revision, Alexis Smith's work provides an often playful, always-meaningful contribution to the chorus of voices lobbying for reexamining and repurposing that dream.

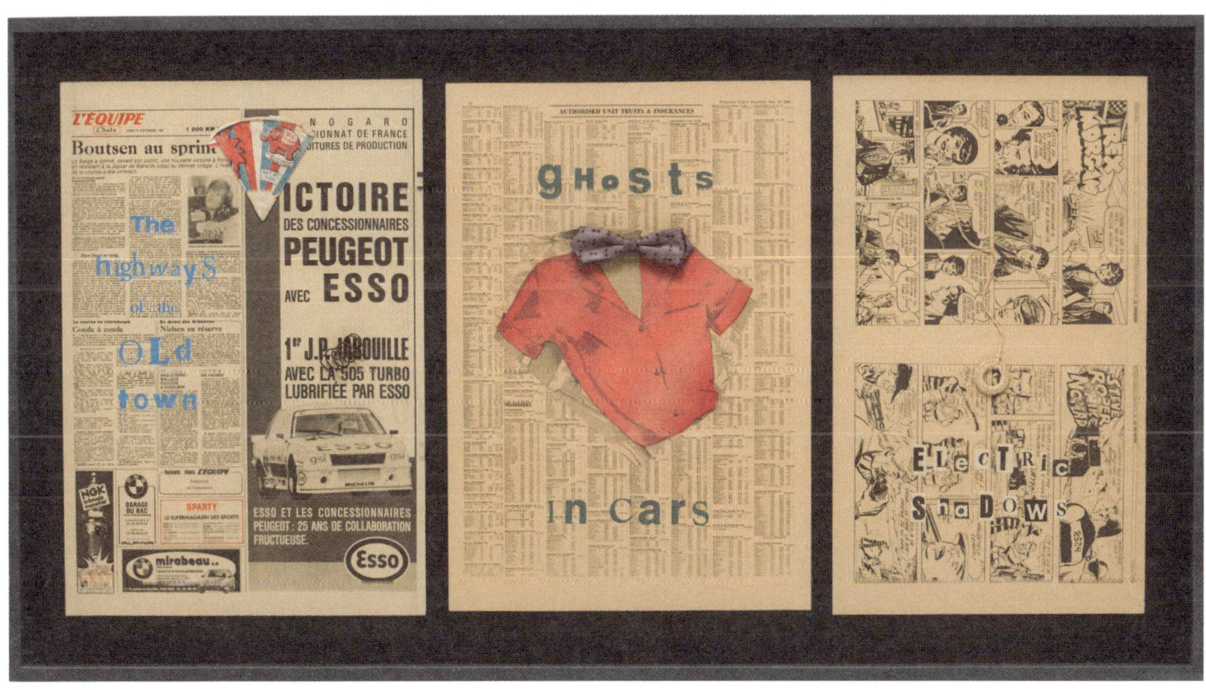

DAILY PLANET, 1986
MIXED MEDIA COLLAGE
TWO PANELS, 28 1/8 x 52" AND 28 1/8 x 51 1/8"
PHOTO ELON SCHOENHOLZ PHOTOGRAPHY
ALL ART COURTESY OF THE ARTIST; IMAGES COURTESY HONOR FRASER GALLERY

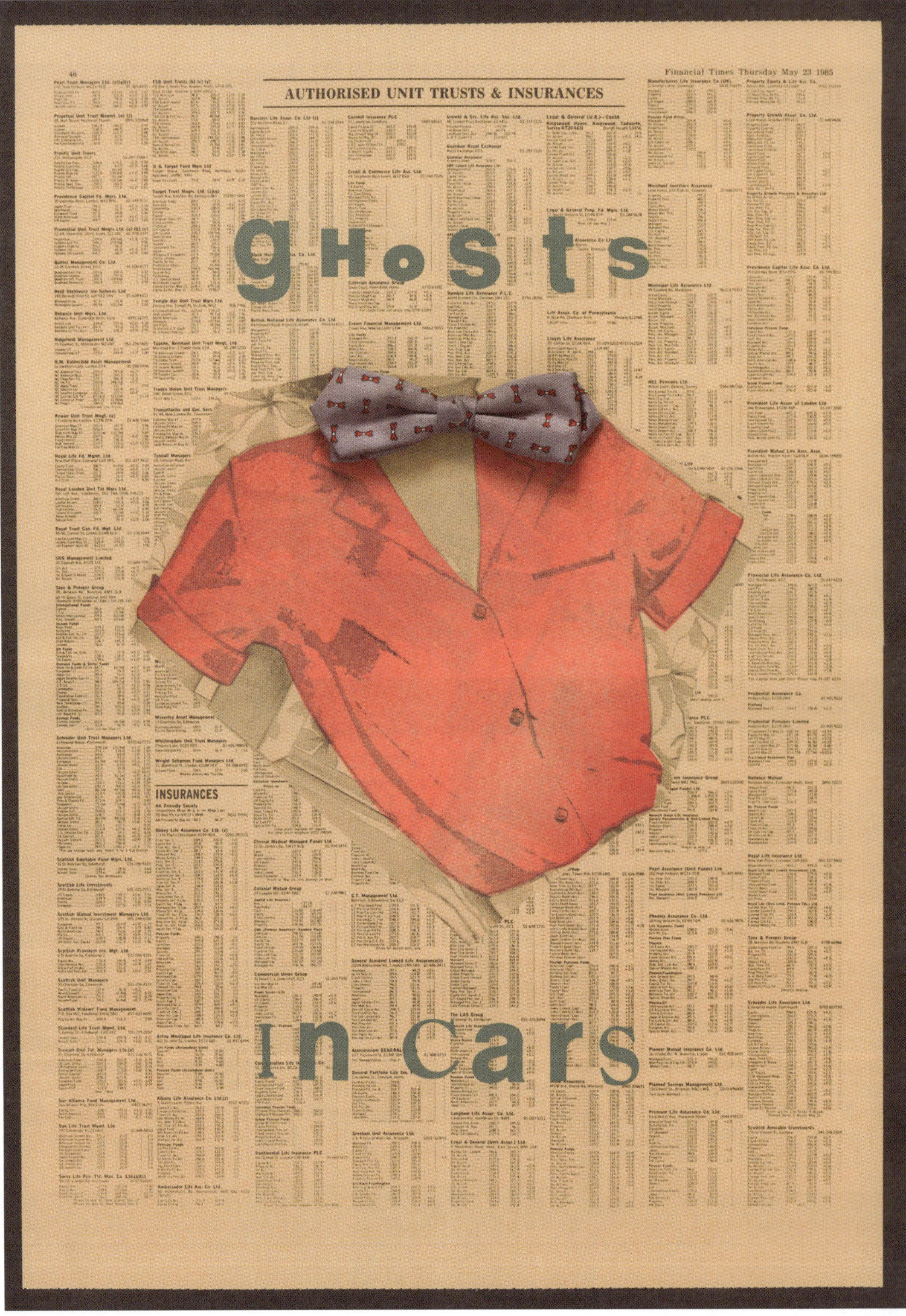

ABOVE AND RIGHT:
DAILY PLANET, 1986
DETAIL

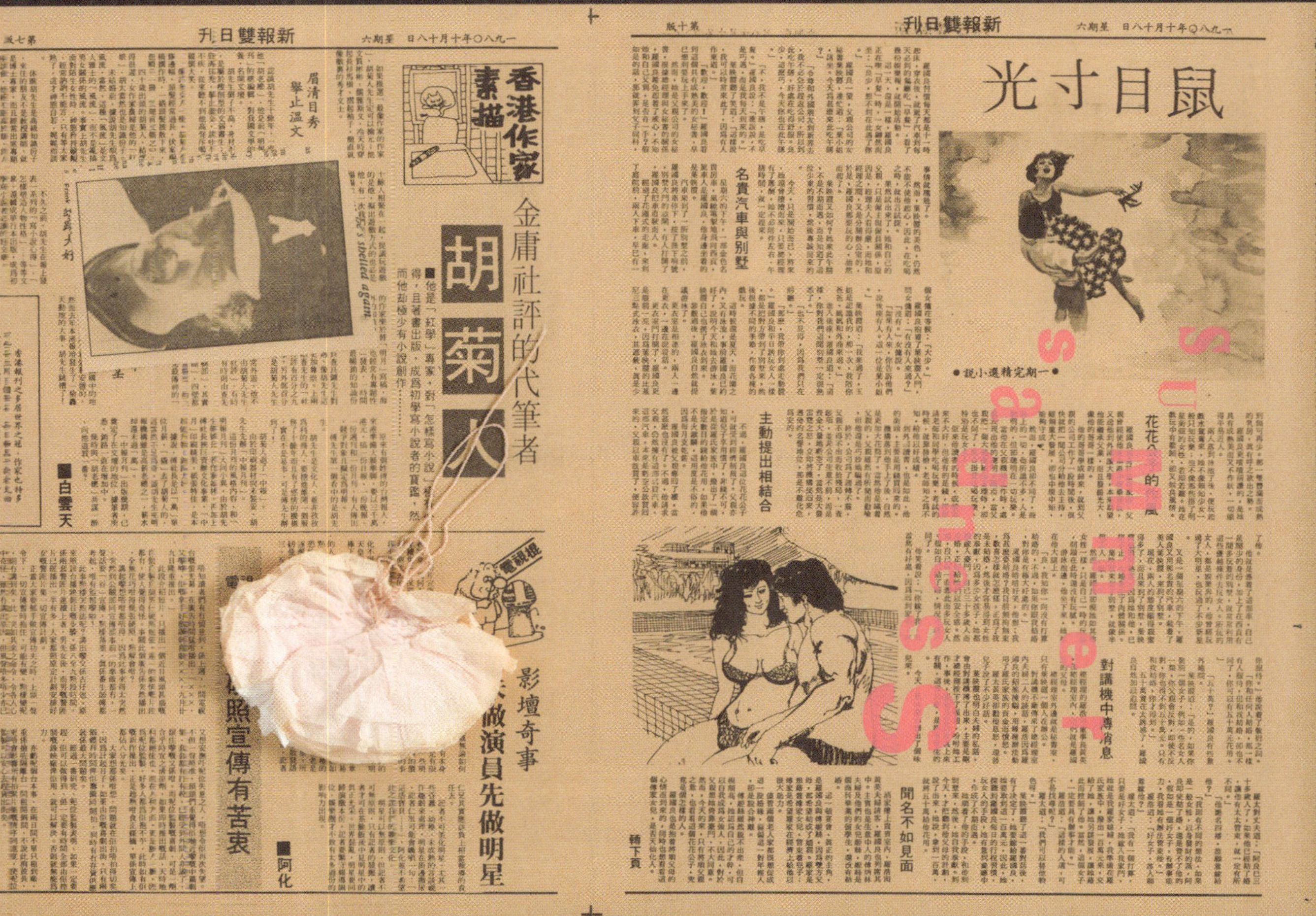

新報雙日刊
鼠目寸光
Summer sadness
主動提出相結合
香港作家素描
金庸社評的代筆者
胡菊人
影壇奇事
未做演員先做明星

THE HUNT, 2013
MIXED MEDIA COLLAGE
TWO PANELS, 31 X 21" EACH

AMERICAN EXPRESS

CHANDLERISM, 1983
MIXED MEDIA COLLAGE, 22 X 14"
PHOTO JOSHUA WHITE/JWPICTURES.COM

LONESOME COWBOY, 2002
MIXED MEDIA COLLAGE
54 1/4 X 40 1/2 X 3"
PRIVATE COLLECTION
IMAGE COURTESY HONOR FRASER GALLERY
PHOTO JOSHUA WHITE/JWPICTURES.COM

HAPPY HUNTING GROUND, 1982
MIXED MEDIA COLLAGE, 17 1/2 x 25 3/4 x 1 5/8"
PHOTO BRIAN FORREST

"Yeah, but you haven't been dead before."

ENLARGED AND IMPROVED SCALE SPECIAL DESIGN REPEATING ACTION
JESSE FRENCH
AND SONS
NEW CASTLE IND.
IF HARMONY IS WHAT YOU CRAVE • THEN GET A TUBA • BURMA-SHAVE

VERMEER DIPTYCH, 2013
MIXED MEDIA COLLAGE
TWO PANELS, 21 1/2 X 17 1/4; 23 X 15"
PHOTO JOSHUA WHITE/JWPICTURES.COM

< *THE PIANO (BURMA-SHAVE #2)*, 2001
MIXED MEDIA
DIMENSIONS VARIABLE
PHOTO BRIAN FORREST

AARP
COMING UP: NEW LOOK, NEW MAGAZINE
MODERN
Maturity
Close Encounters with SHIRLEY MACLAINE
THE RAMBO EXPERIMENT
One Man's Adventure with the New TESTOSTERONE
Ted Koppel
Off Camera
FRANNY
(702) 836-1918
PEPSI

RICHES HAVE WINGS, 2002
MIXED MEDIA COLLAGE
26 1/2 X 24 1/2 X 2 1/2"
PRIVATE COLLECTION
PHOTO JOSHUA WHITE/JWPICTURES.COM

< *DEGREE OF DIFFICULTY*, 2002
MIXED MEDIA COLLAGE
25 1/4 X 20 1/4 X 2 1/4"
COLLECTION OF BROOKE AND ERIK PARKER
PHOTO JOSHUA WHITE/JWPICTURES.COM

FAMILY VALUES, 2009
MIXED MEDIA COLLAGE
THREE PANELS, 31 X 25 X 1"; 27 X 21 X 1 1/2"; 31 X 25 X 1"
COLLECTION OF BRENNA YOUNGBLOOD
PHOTO JOSHUA WHITE/JWPICTURES.COM

CHAPMAN'S
VALENCIAS
OLD MISSION
TRADE MARK
BRAND
THIS FRUIT IS
SCIENTIFICALLY GROWN
AND RIPENED ON THE TREE
SUPERIOR QUALITY
AND UNIFORM GRADE
GROWN IN U.S.A.
REG. U.S. PAT. OFF.
GROWN & SHIPPED BY
PLACENTIA ORCHARD COMPANY
FULLERTON, CALIFORNIA
ORANGE COUNTY
OPERATED UNDER PERSONAL DIRECTION OF
CHARLES C. CHAPMAN
FOR OVER FIFTY YEARS

THE ORANGE INDUSTRIAL COMPLEX

TOM ZOELLNER

ALL FLESH *is as the grass*. This dour wisdom from the Book of Isaiah is also true in reverse: all plants are as flesh. Crops of the fields, like the humans who tend them, have their day and die.

For 70 years, the defining "grass" of Orange County was its namesake product: the sweet fruit that hung from relentless furrows of trees serrating the county from top to bottom. A group of well-off Protestant migrants from the Midwest tried to bring small-farm values to new 19th-century business with the size — and a dose of the heartlessness — of a Southern rice plantation. They managed to create an economy unlike any other in America, as well as a vast tablecloth of waxy leaves, windmills, and dirt farm lanes, all cloaked on chilly mornings in a man-made, frost-defying haze of oily smoke.

The citrus trees left long shadows. Orange County's modern-day fetish for large tracts of single-family homes, the exploitation of Latinos as laborers, the decentered urban carpet, the bland mass culture, the self-conscious expression "California dream," the thirst for youth and cosmetics, the Iowa-like probity: all of these local distinctions can be traced to the time between 1870 and 1950 when the orange was monocultured king, and the local economy arranged around it.

A first irony: oranges aren't native to California. The sweet variety called mandarin emerged in China and Vietnam around the time of Confucius in 500 BCE, then crossed with a related fruit called pomelo. Jews used a hard and sour breed called citron for rituals in the Feast of Tabernacles; the Moors of North Africa are thought to have brought it in the eighth century to Spain, where it softened and sweetened through hybrid speciation to something resembling the Valencias and Washington navels we eat today. During the 15th century, scurvy-wary Spanish sailors brought these seedlings to what is now California, and small groves of sweet oranges were planted on the grounds of the missions that Junípero Serra created in his path up the coast.

But the local birthplace of Orange County's signature business is less picturesque and not even in the county: it's a lonely stretch of Alameda Street south of Fourth Street, at the scruffy edge of downtown Los Angeles, where the only landmarks today are a row of cold-storage seafood warehouses, a weeded-over set of railroad tracks, and a liquor distribution warehouse. No plaque marks the spot where an Anglo trader planted the first set of orange trees for a commercial purpose in Southern California.

That man was William Wolfskill, a Kentucky native who had drifted to Mexico as a mountain man and gotten involved in the frontier liquor business. He and a partner sold jugs of grain alcohol mixed with red pepper and a dash of gunpowder under the name "Taos Lightning" — a booze so vile it could "peel the hide off a Gila Monster," in the words of historian Marshall Trimble. Wolfskill married his way into Mexican citizenship, and while passing through the dusty village of Los Angeles on the way to blaze a trail to the Pacific from Santa Fe, figured that Southern California's climate would support a citrus trade.

He acquired seeds from Serra's 35 trees that grew near the Mission San Gabriel Arcángel and planted them near his farmhouse. There he grew rich exporting his juicy food up the coast by horse cart to the gold-rush camps near Sacramento. By the time of his death in 1866, he owned two-thirds of the orange trees in the state.

Wolfskill's son and business heir Joseph thought even bigger. He understood that local markets were never the future of the California orange; the real money lay in shipping them to places where the fruit was an exotic species, a subject of rumor and fascination. Such was the intention of the first railroad shipment of oranges to St. Louis in 1877, in a single boxcar stacked high with crates stamped "Wolfskill California oranges." In the lore of the California citrus trade, this was like the voyage of the *Discovery*, because new technology was about to make orange growers fantastically rich.

The ice-bunker car, which kept oranges cool with air blown over ice, debuted on the nation's railroad tracks in 1889 — the same year the California Legislature approved the formation of Orange County as a separate political entity, and both the Southern Pacific and the Atchison, Topeka, and Santa Fe feverishly extended their tendrils down to the brand-new farming boomtowns of Anaheim, Orange, and Santa Ana where the land was flat and gloriously empty. Huge fortunes could suddenly be made railing oranges east for customers eager to taste this high-priced exotic dessert.

The Southern Pacific Railroad also doubled-down on hype, popularizing the slogan "Oranges for Health, California for Wealth" and sending promotional trains to state fairs across the Midwest featuring traveling lecturers, glowing booklets, and free samples for locals to enjoy. Unlike heartland cash commodities such as wheat, corn, or oats — nutrient-dense but visually humble grasses — the California orange had an erotic maternal shape, and origins in the sun-splashed Mediterranean instead of gloomy steppes. Citrus sales doubled across the Midwest over the next decade, and some of the new consumers were persuaded to try out the California ranching dream for themselves.

These enterprising landowners tended to be Protestant, wealthy, middle-Western and middle-aged, and looking for a reinvention in the warm sun of a far land. This was, in the words of local antiquarian Charles Fletcher Lummis, "the least heroic migration in history, but the most judicious [...]. [I]nstead of gophering for gold, they planted gold."

The first job of a gentleman orange farmer was finding porous alluvial soil and nearby mountain ranges to provide shelter from restless Santa Ana winds. The best places were known to be immediately southwest of hill slopes, parallel to the wind and resistant to the "frost pockets" of stagnant cold air that could freeze the fruit off a tree in a single night. To best catch the sun's rays, orange seedlings were planted 26 feet apart, in militaristic rows set north-to-south.

He also needed a screen of eucalyptus or poplars to protect the young buds from being blown off the trees in high winds, and cornstalks wrapped around the bases of the trees to protect them from animals.

There had to be a local water cooperative with a system of ditches and canals, run by a foreman — known as a *zanjero* — who kept a strict accounting of when the sluice gates were opened and for how long. He also needed to be patient, because trees didn't grow on trees. They had to be nurtured in seedbeds, carefully planted in rows, and then left to mature for at least six years. But once a tree matured, it produced at least 800 pounds of oranges — 10 boxes worth — which had to be carefully clipped from the branches without nicks that could admit bacteria.

He needed a full complement of the bulbous metal devices known as "smudge pots," which were set on the edges of the groves and set to burn used oil and rubber tires on winter nights so as to create a layer of thick smog over the trees, blanketing them from the bud-killing frost that tended to creep inward. Some of the more well-appointed ranches had electric thermometers in the fields that would set off an alarm inside the house in the middle of the night if the temperature dropped below freezing.

Most importantly of all, he needed a cheap labor base from April to November to pick and sort the fruit if the orchard was big enough. The first field-workers were Chinese or Japanese, many of them former tracklayers who traded in their hammers for a canvas shoulder bag and a tall ladder. They also dammed rivers and dug canals that proved indispensible in the later prosperity of the region. The Chinese, in the words of one approving employer, were "industrious, peaceful, never drank and kept cleaner in body than the Indian did."

Mexican nationals gradually took the place of the Asians. Their wives typically worked in the packinghouses that sat astride the railroad tracks — measuring oranges with metal hoops, washing them in soap and water, treating the greenish ones with ethylene gas to warm their color, wrapping the fleshy spheres in thin paper stamped with a brand label, and arranging them into wooden crates plastered with colorful labels idealizing and eroticizing their own image and labor: buxom young women cradling sacks full of equally voluptuous oranges, against a backdrop of snowy mountain peaks and the spires of semi-ruined Catholic churches. The caricatures were so resplendent that many of these labels were framed and hung as artwork in distant living rooms.

The real life of the Latino fruit-picker or packer, of course, was not so picturesque. Wages were about two cents per box picked, and workers lived in rows of squalid shacks next to the canals. Orange resident Ken Schlueter, whose father owned 625 trees in the city when he was growing up in the 1950s, recalled being sent out to work alongside the Mexican crews, his well-to-do father's way of imparting a work ethic. They would bring him homemade tacos that they had heated up with hot coals buried inside the earth. He always felt outdone on the ladders, for his co-workers were rapid and precise, fleecing each tree from the top on down, making the oranges rain down to the earth in a cannonade of soft thuds. "Their hands were in constant motion," he told me. Harvesting oranges was a far more labor-intensive enterprise than stripping an Iowa farm of corn and wheat. "One acre here took as much work as a hundred acres in the Midwest," said Schlueter.

In brand-new settlements like Pasadena, Pomona, Riverside, Orange, and Santa Ana, the transplanted citrus elite like the Schlueters and their families found a "new El Dorado" and built Victorian houses, libraries, churches, and small opera houses — recreating the cities of a more established America, according to familiar patterns. A group of German immigrants from Ohio founded St. John's Lutheran Church in the city of Orange and built a pink and gray Gothic Revival sanctuary in 1913 that would have looked entirely at home in a cozy suburb of Cincinnati. The citrus trade was, said William Andrew Spalding, "an industry suited to the most intelligent and refined people."

But instead of seas of wheat or corn around them, there were phalanxes of the fragrant trees — once viewed as a romantic gift of the Spanish padres, produced now for the more Yankee virtues of thrift, industry, and bulk commodities. Orange County became, in the words of historian Phil Brigandi, "one vast orchard, dotted with little towns." Folded between the chain of tourist villages on the Pacific Coast and the range of the Santa Ana Mountains to the east, the county was a matrix of groves, dirt roads, windmills, and canals: "wall-to-wall trees," in the recollections of Ken Schlueter.

The Santa Fe and Southern Pacific Railroads, hubbed in Los Angeles around a mini-city of cold storage warehouses, linked this archipelago society of sweet fruit to the rest of the country. The polycentric foundations of modern Southern California were laid down through this interconnection between the orchards and their bulk storage, a network that would later provide the essential skeleton of the modern freeway system.

Typical among the Tom Sawyers who arrived for Orange County's second act was Charles C. Chapman, who had been an ambitious young seller of apples next to the railroad tracks in his Illinois hometown. He later operated a telegraph and had gotten rich off writing and publishing local histories across the Midwest. At the age of 41, he moved to warm Los Angeles for his wife's health and bought a "sadly neglected" grove near Placentia, almost as a hobby. When he wanted to visit it, he rode the Santa Fe Railroad to Fullerton — a town where he would later become the Republican mayor — and peddled his bicycle eight miles out to the oranges.

What made him atypical was his willingness to take creative risks in crop cultivation and sales. Chapman figured out that, unlike the Washington navel oranges which dominated the business, Valencia oranges could be left on the trees an extra six months after ripening and then shipped east in August — a season in which buyers were not accustomed to seeing oranges.

He also cut down on spoilage by insisting that his pickers wear leather gloves and cut the stems with rounded-tip clippers in such a way as not to leave small gashes that eventually harbored mold and could spoil an entire crate. After he shipped an initial carload of fruit back East at the end of the summer of 1897 — a rail voyage that recreated Joseph Wolfskill's famous shipment to St. Louis — he made a huge profit and Valencia orange trees soon took over the inner folds of the coastal plains.

Chapman created a brand with an especially sumptuous crate label, featuring a ridiculous fantasy landscape of snowy peaks, palm trees, cactus, and, in the foreground, a group of portly Catholic monks inspecting a freshly picked orange with amazement and delight. *Scientifically grown*, proclaimed the advertising. The iconography and the brand name, Old Mission, were plucked directly from the hype surrounding the novel *Ramona* by Helen Hunt Jackson, which told the story of a mixed-race Indian girl growing up on a ranchero. The romantic portrayal sparked a touristic craze for Southern California and its vanilla-Mexican curios.

Chapman's fame grew in this atmosphere. The trade press ran fawning stories on him, and one editor offered him $50,000 cash for the privilege of selling oranges for two years under the Old Mission brand. (Chapman declined the offer.) "He is indeed the ORANGE KING, not only of America but also of the world," proclaimed the *Fruit Trade Journal* in 1905. Chapman molded himself into a Southern California version of Ben Franklin, making himself both eminently useful to those around him and phenomenally rich.

Chapman joined the boards of hospitals, banks, and Christian missionary societies, married a pretty young second wife from the church choir, got himself elected mayor of Fullerton, founded a newspaper, and built a rambling 13-room mansion. He even persuaded the Santa Fe Railroad to build a branch line out to his orchard. Despite never having gone to college himself, he put forward nearly half a million dollars in a nationwide fundraising challenge to revive the fortunes of a moribund Bible school and rebrand it as Chapman College (a name he swore was chosen by the trustees without his knowledge). His interest in Christian education was topped only by a young orange farmer named Charles Fuller, who used the oil-drilling royalties from his orchard in Placentia to put himself through Bible school. Fuller went on to a career as an international radio evangelist as the host of *The Old-Fashioned Revival Hour* and founded the influential Fuller Theological Seminary.

Chapman's own evangelism on progress and American values was a regular crowd-pleaser at the California Valencia Orange Show, a kitschy 1920s fair called a "fairyland of fruit" by the *Santa Ana Daily Register*. The child-friendly show embodied much of the exuberance and goofiness of the Jazz Age: fake Arabic minarets, models wearing bathing suits, high towers of fruit, parades and floats, congratulatory phone calls from the president of the United States.

This fair was the public face of the California Fruit Growers Exchange, a powerful oligarchy that functioned as a seller's ring. Independent farming had never worked out very well in Orange County. In the early days, a grower had no choice but to sell his crop to any number of agents representing the packinghouses who would estimate a price based on what they saw on the trees — and this price was often a result of collusion. Some Orange County growers were persuaded to sell their fruit on consignment, which meant that if it showed up in Chicago as spoiled pulpy mush, they got nothing in return. Brokers could also falsify their spoilage reports and deal contraband oranges on the black market.

Fed up with the disorganized system, a number of powerful growers formed the California Fruit Growers Exchange in 1905 to share packinghouses, codify grading standards, and stabilize prices. It functioned like a nonprofit, owning no property and selling no shares, but it commanded enormous power, employed a national network of salesmen, and paid huge telegraph bills. They pooled the annual crops of Washington navels and Valencias from various districts around Southern California and sold them in bulk. Train schedules and deliveries were coordinated out of a high-gated office on Glassell Street in downtown Orange that looked more like a Middle Eastern temple than a place of business.

Despite the pro–small business rhetoric of most growers, this was not lassiez-faire economics at work, nor did it really resemble a Jeffersonian democracy of small landholders. This was, in the words of historian Laura Gray Turner, the essence of "managerial corporate capitalism." Led by a dapper ex–US Department of Agriculture man named G. Harold Powell, the exchange functioned as a legal monopoly that happened to be exempt from antitrust laws; fewer than 200 men owned plots of more than 100 acres. The Orange County elite made the decisions and controlled the prices.

Charles Chapman was one of the notable holdouts: he feared the brand power of Old Mission would be diluted if he had to sell through a single channel. But like the CFGE, he was not above bending the rules of free enterprise and engaging in outright market manipulation. "It was early evident that California citrus could not, without protection, successfully compete with foreign fruit, especially from Italy and Spain," he wrote in his autobiography.

In 1908, Chapman and several associates lobbied the House Ways and Means committee for a one-cent-per-pound tariff on European oranges, which opened up the ports of Boston and New York to his higher-priced goods. And when he got news of a shipment coming across the Atlantic in spite of the stiff duties, he played hardball. "When a consignment of foreign fruit came into the harbor and was offered for sale, a sufficient amount of our fruit was offered on the market to depress it or break it" — usually about 100 train cars "donated to be sacrificed on these markets." Like a generation of 19th-century monopolists before him, Chapman and his allies also pressured the railroads for special-rate deals. When the tariff again came up for reconsideration in 1913, Chapman

made a special plea for the "fostering care that our Government has always been good enough to give new industries." California thus muscled its way into Eastern iceboxes.

The rise of the CFGE and the era of Big Fruit came with a wave of orchard consolidation and the end of the "gentleman farmer" way of life in Orange County. Yet it ordered the market in times of uncertainty, created new year-round markets, and made large investments a little safer. Oranges were still a notional product, ranking nearly as frivolous and childlike as candy. There were up to five million orange trees in Southern California by that time, serving a national appetite that could turn fickle at any moment.

In the early decades of the 20th century, Orange County faced an imbalance dreaded by every manufacturer: an overabundance of product not matched by rising demand. The ad agency of Lord & Thomas — and its in-house poets — dreamed up a campaign to boost sales that played off popular fear. The disaster of the Spanish Flu epidemic during World War I had made Americans more germ-conscious than ever. But the pasteurization process had recently made it possible to rid a beverage of bacteria.

Lord & Thomas came up with the simple slogan "Drink an Orange" to promote the simple but excitingly novel idea of having a glass of juice at breakfast — adding a morning eating ritual, in liquid form, which had been practically unknown before. Breakfast was "a habit meal," said the agency, not prone to much variance from day to day. And in that morning ritual was the possibility

— if not the expectation — of daily consumption of a fruit thus far regarded as a dessert delicacy. "Its delicious juice is as invigorating as it is palatable," said Charles Chapman in one of his many speeches, "giving to man increased nerve power and a clear brain."

Orange County's liquid product took on the name of an earlier CFGE brand called "Sunkist," which evoked in a single phrase what had been portrayed in all the kitschy art on all the wooden crates over the years. The name graced billboards across the nation, educational films passed out to public schools, huge neon displays in Times Square and Coney Island. "Thanks to admen," wrote historian Jared Farmer, "the sweet orange completed its trajectory from fruit of the gods to the aristocracy to the bourgeoisie to the average Joe." Vitamin C would not be isolated in a laboratory and clearly understood until 1932, but the mysteriously healthful qualities of orange juice were all over the press.

The word Sunkist became so popular that the CFGE adopted it as the new name for the organization and stamped it directly on the oranges in black ink. Oranges, and orange juice, had found their direct competition not in other fruits but in sugared beverages like 7 Up and Coca-Cola, and Sunkist found its marketing strategy in the bright colors and salutary qualities of its product. Though it was not fizzy, it emerged from nature and not from the bottling plant. The advertising for Sunkist got so thick, wrote historian Douglas Cazaux Sackman, that nearly 1,500 Manhattan retail stores and soda fountains had bright orange advertisements plastered in their windows. At Christmas, a cartoon Santa Claus offered an orange as the "most *healthful* gift."

Some of the local connotations of "Sunkist" were not nearly as radiant. In 1936, more than 2,000 *naranjeros* decided they had had enough of poor working conditions and put down their round-tipped clippers in an attempt to strike. But their uprising was doomed from the start. The local press, including *The Santa Ana Register*, portrayed them as disloyal saboteurs similar to the IWW Wobblies who had tried to organize factories around the time of the outbreak of World War I. According to historian and journalist Gustavo Arellano, one of the pickers bit a policeman's arm, Mexican strikers were thrown in jail, and the Orange County sheriff gave "shoot to kill" orders, deputizing American Legion members to guard the orchards with shotguns. Hecklers broke up union meetings and police threw tear gas canisters through the windows.

The lawyer and journalist Carey McWilliams was appalled at the head-cracking he witnessed and coined the term "Gunkist" to describe the danger and violence roiling in the sun-splashed orchards. "Under the direction of Sheriff Logan Jackson, who should long be remembered for his brutality in this strike, over 400 special guards, armed to the hilt, are conducting a terroristic campaign of unparalleled ugliness," McWilliams wrote in *Pacific Weekly*. In the end, growers agreed only to minimal wage hikes and no union.

As labor tensions reached fever pitch, the California orange empire was already wilting from a series of cultural and economic blows. The colorful crate labels had begun to shed their fanciful Raphaelite iconography in favor of the simple word "Sunkist" across a blue background; with the advent of chain groceries and cardboard boxes in the 1950s, the crates themselves became a memory. Tired of the industry's smog — even uglier and more pervasive than the growing encroachment of car exhaust — municipalities all over the Southland began outlawing the smudge pots lit aflame on the edges of orchards on cold nights. A disease with the poetically clinical name of "quick decline" ran through the orchards, turning trees into dead sticks within a week. The blight spread through the ground, traveling root to root, and one sick tree could ruin all of its neighbors. Ken Schlueter recalled digging deep trenches around healthy trees, trying to keep them from dying.

And the most unstoppable force of all, even worse than quick decline: newly prosperous young couples sought detached ranch homes — a slice of the California good life — for themselves in the peace and prosperity in the early 1950s. Ten acres of orange trees started looking like a sucker bet compared to 40 new houses on quarter-acre lots. Schlueter's father gave in and sold out after the city incorporated his property and raised his taxes.

In 1953, the movie studio chief Walt Disney acquired 160 acres of orange and walnut trees on Harbor Boulevard, right off the new Santa Ana freeway, with more profitable ideas than agriculture. The Stanford Research Institute had studied land growth patterns and real estate models and told him the spot was an ideal place for a new amusement park, whose design was based on a railroad fair that Disney had seen in Chicago five years prior. The bulldozers went to work on the morning of July 16, 1954, and the rise of Disneyland on a vanished bed of citrus was the highest-profile land conversion yet of what had already become an unstoppable change.

Within a decade, the citrus business hastened its move to the Central Valley, near towns like Visalia and Tulare, where land could be bought for a fifth of the cost. Orange County became a residential instead of agricultural satellite of greater Los Angeles — celebrating its namesake crop with bas-relief concrete displays on the noise-dimming walls of the Garden Grove Freeway, and a few remaining acres of symbolic trees that historical preservationists had to fight to keep. The "fruit frost service" reports disappeared from KFI radio.

Only locals who know what to look for today can see the faintly visible archaeology of the orange empire — from the Anaheim Orange & Lemon Association Packing House turned into a food court, to the Santiago Orange Growers Association building on a quiet street near the railroad tracks, waiting for Chapman University to find a re-adaptive use for it.

Orange County's dominant industry lasted 70 years — which the Bible holds to be about the natural lifespan of a human being, the metaphorical flesh. It ultimately succumbed to the changing technologies of agriculture and the shifting economies of real estate that spelled a natural fate for the plantations. The same forces, in other words, that helped create them.

While the trunks of the last orange trees were burned and mulched decades ago, they left imprints that go deeper than the name of the county or the bulbous image on its seal. The echoing imprint of the citrus business can be perceived in the rectangular tract subdivisions that match the acreage of the orchards they replaced; within the segregated neighborhoods of Anaheim and Santa Ana, where the Latino grandchildren of the *naranjeros* live on the disadvantaged side of a racial rift as pronounced as anywhere in the Deep South; within the volubly conservative editorial page of the *Orange County Register*, within the cultural emphasis on overt displays of wealth and youthful voluptuousness as fetishized and misleading as any rural maiden pictured on a crate label.

Critics of Orange County look at the orchard-sized subdivisions, or the vast consumerist rectangle of South Coast Plaza, the smoked-glass office parks with grassy berms and bottlebrush trees out front, the chintzy Spanish Mission architectural vocabulary, the feeder avenues as wide as rivers, and declare the whole scene bland, monotonous, and corporate. But so were the orange plantations they replaced, if not more so.

A common tourist habit is to imagine what the scene might have looked like in a previous era, especially in older parts of the world. How did the coast of Virginia look to those English sailors, for example, or the cliffs of Capri to a Roman solider? This exercise is especially difficult in Orange

County's flat parts when you try to see through the wide-boulevard monoculture of Del Taco and Ralphs into a time not yet a century ago, when the roads were all dirt and the sun was blocked out by a mathematically precise forest of orange and lemon trees.

The trees are all gone now — *sic transit gloria citrus* — but they molded the county into what it is today, in the aspects we celebrate, and also those held up as regional jokes or stereotypes. There's a reflexive tendency to think of our orange-ranching era in a golden light, perhaps because of the lost ethic of physical work or the pleasing taste of the fruit, but the reality was often contradictory and difficult. So it's important not just to envision the vanished trees but to see them for what they really were.

Near the center of the college that Charles Chapman helped endow, and where I now teach, is a statue of our founder seated in an easy chair. He leans slightly forward as if telling a story or giving a piece of advice. A dwarf orange tree grows behind him. Carved on the back of this memorial are words from his autobiography, which describe the business strategy that vaulted him to prominence:

> I knew from experience that there were periods when citrus fruits were entirely absent from markets in the East, and I believed that if I could get oranges to customers during those periods I might develop a really profitable trade. So I took my courage in my hands and delayed any Valencia picking until long after all the other varieties had gone. Then we shipped [our oranges on] our first experimental [railroad] cars. The response was beyond my greatest expectations. The "trade" eagerly accepted this new variety, which was solid, juicy, long-keeping and delicious.

Words on stone monuments are not usually so practical and specific. But this inscription perfectly symbolizes what the promise of Orange County represented for an earlier generation. Civilizations both great and small are founded more on economic schemes than high moral purpose, which comes as an afterthought.

For 70 years, Orange County once stood for the harnessing of nature, the manipulation of distant capital markets, the production of sensual pleasure, the unapologetic mythologizing of an abundance not shared by all (especially those who picked the fruit), enjoyment of material success, the dependence on the Lord's constant blessings of warm sun, cheap land, and frost-free air. It was a place that its citrus lords perceived to be free of history, leaving them free to make their own. This is the orange-ghosted world we live in today.

This essay will appear in the forthcoming anthology The Barricades of Heaven: A Literary Field Guide to Orange County, California, *to be published by Heyday in 2017.*

Death KIM YOUNG

After *Memorial Photo: Self-Portrait* by Robert Delford Brown

SINCE WE CAN see the eyes, the second set, just below the normal eyes that would appear in the normal spot of the photograph — but it's this second set coming through, the little holes torn in the paper. And then the red paint — not brushed, but smeared over the entire portrait, as if to erase this image of a man in a thin tie and trimmed moustache, as if there was something else animating him, something that comes through, that must come through.

If you know anything about Robert Delford Brown (and I admit I know very little), it's that his art — the overlay, the underlay, the paint, and the little holes for eyes — is really about what might never be known. They call him a visionary, but his brilliance seems to be a sort of gleeful acceptance of what one can never see.

The First National Church of the Exquisite Panic, Inc. — his church — worships a deity called "Who" ("What does the future hold? Who knows") and, according to *The New York Times* obit, is centered around a philosophy called "Pharblongence" — meaning confused.

Sure, craftwise, eyes, eye color, windows of the soul — all that — means very little. But I'm interested here in what the eyes, the second set, say about not knowing.

I imagine Brown making the second eyes — tearing the paper and then smearing the paint over the photo. It's not that you don't care anymore, but you forget the critical analysis of composition — and then you do it. Mar the thing. Mar the thing you think you know best. This is art. When you're willing to fuck it up.

My four-year-old daughter spends hours with her markers on her knees drawing over the book she made the day before. She walks down the hall telling stories of Mira, the transgendered bat who becomes a he-princess, and Orangu, who eats plants out in the black garden of a night. Art is what you make when you know you can't know. When we first told her about someone dying, she asked us, yelled, demanded: "But where do you go!?!? Where. Do. You. Go."

Ask the second set of eyes.

DWYER KILCOLLIN
EMERGENT OBJECT: CHAIR I, 2014
RESIN AND STONE WITH STEEL ARMATURE
34 X 17 X 20", UNIQUE
COURTESY OF THE ARTIST AND M+B GALLERY

MICHAEL WAUGH, *ALCHEMY (FCIR, PART 6)*, 2015
INK ON MYLAR, 42 X 65", COURTESY OF THE ARTIST AND VON LINTEL GALLERY

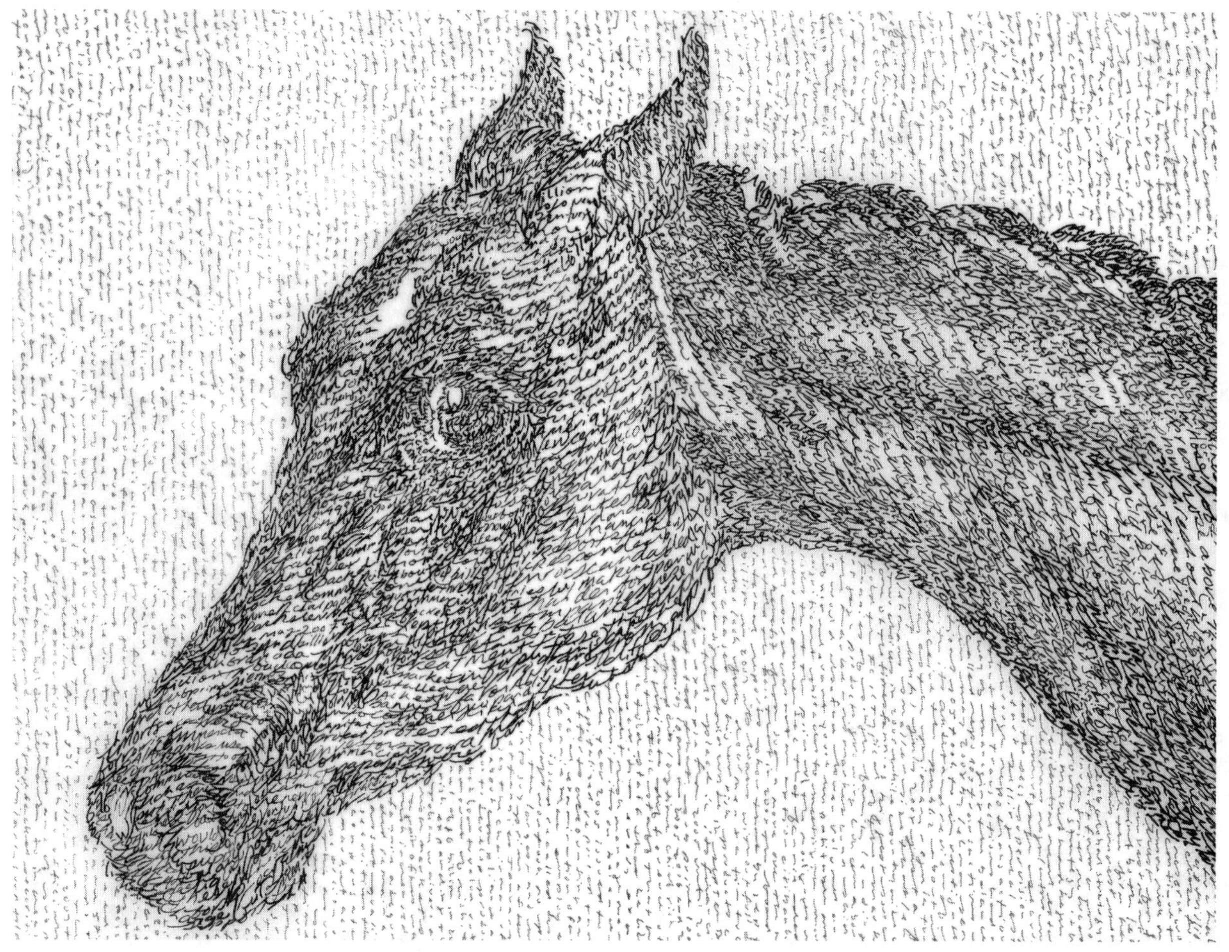

MICHAEL WAUGH
ALCHEMY (FCIR, PART 6), (DETAIL)

Eden: A Postscript

NATALIE EILBERT

This kind of living is interesting. Interact with the symbols
of confession, erupt from exhaustion. Human toil
improves the whiteness of my eyes. I deep-fry a tooth
in marrow oil, chew it into a paste, smear it over your hole.
I made you to be better, but from my spit you were the same.
You stalked the long grass, grinned your violence into absolution.
You moved your stick limbs, fluttered your lips
into a rounder pronoun. You're relearning language
to become yourself again, fathered by the smoke of my history.
This is what you wanted. This exercise turned compendium:
what male figure was worse, impacted my jowls, pushed
pyrite through my nostril to imbue my tongue fresh metals.
I would like to rectify something, if I may. You "let me
off the hook" when I couldn't produce fast enough a list of men.
I admitted perhaps I was wrong about what happened.
I coughed a gold pebble into my palm and stared at its beautiful
shine. I am amazed at your courage, all of you who have told me
my mistakes were the wrong mistakes. But I articulated perfectly
at a reading why failure is so important to me. There was
a failure done / to me first, and so I grant failure the way light
grants a prism. What if I told you that I enjoyed it at the time.
I was seven. Or I was six. I was thirteen. I was fourteen.
I was twenty-three. Would you disabuse me. I told you already my alibi
is a pool party, locked eyes, a shirt pulled overhead. I told you
it's acrylic blue on cheap paper and it never dries. It's important
that you called me a liar. I blinked seeds into a shape.
Every memory is an offense to what happened. You leaned me
over a couch gripping my cunt, isn't that right. You said
Is this what you want, and I wept, for I was finally found.

A Valley Is Where a Hole Ends and We Are Forced to Begin

NATALIE EILBERT

I don't know what I am. A valley opens in my chest in bed
and then I'm googling "yoga poses for panic attacks." The woman
in her pink lululemon pants folded neatly in Big Toe Pose.
So badly I need to fold over and so badly was I folded over.
A valley is a hole with mountain privileges. A valley is a hole
made of gentle edges, insidious and thriving.
This is the paradox to any surface. I breathe on this surface.
Can't suck in air. Not enough. Numb limbs. Bad pulse.
How many valleys open in how many chests every day.
In the valley a masked man walks to me. He breathes deeply.
In the room I'm alone. I have always been alone. Ribs knit.
I don't know what it's like to be a citizen but I am welcome. I spoke to the ceiling
my abuses all these years. I spoke to my ceiling tonight as I fucked.
Why were there always people in the next room. I speak to the ceiling.
I'll tell you my biggest fear it's figures standing in darkness.
We were given bodies to be alone in, if we were given anything.
To understand singularity we sit inside it. More than anything we sit inside it.
To my left is no figure standing in the darkness. My shape folds neatly to move
away from my shape. I sit inside it. Rabbit. Fear is somebody waiting for me
to notice them as I wait to not notice them. Rabbit. I don't think loss is different.
Why were there always people in the next room. Why does it feel like
someone handed me a token when they ripped the clothes from my shape.
I fold neatly to move away from my shape. Fish Pose. Bow Pose. I turn
the lights on. Rabbit. No one is here. I speak to tear through. Lie down.

MICHAEL WAUGH
SHADOW BANKING (FCIR, PART 3), (DETAIL), 2015
INK ON MYLAR
25 X 25"
COURTESY OF THE ARTIST AND VON LINTEL GALLERY

Liquid Waste

NATALIE EILBERT

Drip. Something mildews. Now when I have no prompt
but concept I stain the mattress with concept. I plump from
the fatty folds of excess thought. I was born with black eyes
open, meaning I peeled back slick and stared through vaginal light.
I was given a name, my slime-wet rock yawned new technology.
Did I earn new status when he shouldn't have ______, I did not.
My carriage spills cheap fuel. Something mildews. A stranger
follows me up the stairs of my building. I tell him to leave.
He tells me he'd like to come in. My door leaks a hundred suns.
L'esprit de l'escalier means staircase wit, a comeback conceived of
after the event. I say the words leave on the staircase without wit,
panic yellow in my mouth, the staircase spirals to the infinite
as invectives bleed from my teeth. What is this phrase then,
how do its words actualize event and discourse. I see the stairs
eidetic behind closed eyes, his begging face, and the miracle
of his turning away to leave. Yes yes I darken with excess thought,
I fat out words from my throat, I stroke the cheek of a wall
as I fill with vinegar. What else can I be today but gratuitous
language in open air. How else can this end but with spilling.
Hundreds of dead moons spilt from my hundreds of cunts.
It's not that he shouldn't have. I chase these beasts into a spiral
to the infinite stairs, pull fur from my lips. How cheap. ///

< DWYER KILCOLLIN
TABLEAU (FRAMED ON BIAS), 2016
RESIN, STONE, AND STAINLESS STEEL
18 3/4 X 15 X 4 3/4", UNIQUE
COURTESY OF THE ARTIST AND M+B GALLERY

CITY (NOT) ON FIRE

MICHAEL J. AGOVINO

IN 1977, WE PLAYED BALL. *We played basketball, handball, stickball, stickball barely still a thing. We invented shit, punch ball, slap ball, off-the-wall (before the record came out), chuck ball, like stickball but with the bat of a nunchuck.*

We were too young, just kids, but we watched the older guys play touch football in the street (three completions for a first down), maneuvering, showing off, around the blue MTA buses, the Bx15, the Bx17, the W in the WBLS ad always sideways, the orange bus to Queens, and the Manhattan express buses. There was this sweet music that always played, if not the Stylistics anymore — all that longing in falsetto, "write your name across the sky …," *no, that was old, from kindergarten — it was Tavares still or L.T.D. Already we liked to dance.*

We were white, we were black, we were half-white half-black, we were white wanting to be black, black wanting to be white. We were Puerto Rican. There were two Indian kids, from India; they were down. We were ahead of our time; if only we'd known. No one particularly cared.

We had fights, play fights, during school, after school. We went to school together, public school. We got stuck in the elevators together; there was piss in the elevators, and in the stairwells. We took the stairwells together, in pairs, those dark stairwells filled with smashed fluorescent lights, graffiti even on the banisters. We took buses to the RKO Fordham together, to the White Castle on Gun Hill Road.

We were skinny, and we were fast, God, were we fast — yo, that boy can book! *— and we never knew when we'd have to run. There were stray Dobermans from Boston Road, kids from the Valley, from Section 5, teenagers from Truman.*

This was 1977. Or was it '76? You can say '78. We were scared but we didn't show it.

There's a scene, a brief one, in *Stations of the Elevated*, Manfred Kirchheimer's sublime, suddenly timely 1981 film of a New York City on its knees — released quietly late last year digitally and as a limited-edition DVD from Oscilloscope — that if you hadn't grown up in the city would mean nothing. It begins as a loving exterior shot of a slow-moving graffiti-covered subway car on one of the elevated lines in the Bronx. Then, in the foreground, a bus bursts through the perfectly framed composition.

It's not one of the dozens of MTA city buses, not the Bx this, the B or Q that. It is, instead, a red, white, and blue coach, a private line, the seats cushioned, the windows tinted, that coursed between Manhattan and the Bronx, north, northeast, to neighborhoods not only without cachet, that much was a given — it was the Bronx after all, besides Riverdale, what cachet? — but to mysterious outskirts that may well have not existed. (Was it Throggs Neck or Throgs Neck? Where, in God's name, did the Sheridan Expressway begin? Where did it end? Was it Co-op or Co-Op City? And anyway, we, who lived there, just called it Co-op. Were they even co-ops? *Yo, any a y'all been to Parkchester? It's like Co-op?* Even we didn't know the answers.)

Those bus lines (New York Bus Service was the name of the company) started in the early 1970s, with the city broke and broken down, the subway system being the most conspicuous emblem. The buses traveled far and wide up the Bruckner Expressway, often to the dreaded two-fare zones, meaning to get to the subway, if you rode them — and some people chose not to — you had to take a bus and, without a free transfer, pay double.

The subways in those years, no matter how mesmerizing they are now, and were then to some — to Kirchheimer to Martin Wong to Norman Mailer — could also be terrifying. Sometimes the fear was imagined; other times it wasn't. (Mailer lived within the cul-de-sac of Brooklyn Heights, and his left hook, no matter how well practiced at the Gramercy Boxing Gym, would've had a tough time scoring against younger, quicker opposition with switchblades on the Elder Avenue platform.) The subways were slow, dirty, loud. They'd come whenever. The lights would go out for a few beats, maybe a full measure. Guys would ride between cars, why it wasn't clear. The last car was off-limits. The feeling was that anything could happen at any time.

So New York Bus Service thrived — during rush hour the driver might declare "standing room only, standing room only" — and one of its fleet interrupts, for a moment, the filmmaker's compassionate gaze. Kirchheimer's film, though shown at the 1981 New York Film Festival, was soon forgotten. By the end of the decade, most of the graffiti was covered with a putrid, life-sucking maroon paint, the ensuing cars dubbed "the red birds." *Stations* was a rumor more than anything, until excerpts of it appeared at the Museum of the City of New York in 2014 as part of the exhibit *City as Canvas: Graffiti Art from the Martin Wong Collection* and then showed at the Brooklyn Academy of Music.

There are no interviews in the film, no narration. The only voices are those of children from the Central and South Bronx. They're sweet-faced kids, without much to do except play amid the building carcasses and admire the subway expressionism, lowercase *e*, sans art world endorsement; no Neo-Pop Expressionism in these parts. The kids speak like we spoke: "Check it out, that shit is bad"; "that Slave piece was def, man, that dude is bustin' out." (What happened to those kids? How did life treat them? Are they okay?)

In place of talking heads, Kirchheimer uses music. Not Bongo Rock or the Jimmy Castor Bunch, nor the emerging sound of the Cold Crush Brothers, Grandmaster Flash, or Kurtis Blow, who by the mid-'80s would migrate to Co-op, our neighbor, but instead Charles Mingus — "Better Git It In Your Soul"; "Haitian Fight Song"; "Fables of Faubus" — with a touch of Aretha at the end.

Mingus's music is somehow perfectly New York in all its paradoxes: brawling but refined; angry but graceful; highly composed but improvisational; melancholy but triumphant. (And anyway, Mingus and Danny Richmond kept way better time than the MTA.)

Kirchheimer sees the ironies. (German-born, New York City–raised after fleeing the Nazis, he seems most enchanted with the No. 5 train.) High on billboards, sanctioned painters stencil in advertisements, smiling white faces with blue eyes, selling products — cigarettes, suntan lotion, hamburgers — to be appropriated, any day, by Richard Prince, et al., and sold in burgeoning SoHo. In one three-car succession, there is a mural of the Bicentennial, followed in the next car by "Heaven Is Life," and in the very next "Earth Is Hell," enveloped with flames.

New York City from that era, and the Bronx particularly, had a Dante-esque quality. A little *Paradiso* — all those Catholic schools (oy), Hayes, Spellman, Tolentine, Mount Saint Michael, Stepinac, Fordham University, Manhattan College; *The Angel Esmeralda*, by the Bronx's own bard; and lest we forget, Mount Hope and Mount Eden (if only) — though more celebrated for *Inferno*: *The Bronx Is Burning*; *Love Goes to Buildings on Fire*; last October's *Macabre Suite*, a pop-up art exhibit and party with Melo and a Jenner and developers trying to rebrand Mott Haven "the Piano District"; and the recent novel *City on Fire*, which earned the author, Garth Risk Hallberg, $2 million, quadruple what Reggie was paid in 1977, '76 too, and probably '78, even after going deep three times in Game 6.

—

In 1979, we bought sneakers. PRO-Keds were wack now, you had to have Clydes or shell tops. You had to hook them up with thick laces, double laces, or the checkerboard. If they were white, you polished them with Sani-White; if they were suede, you kept them fresh with a toothbrush. You kept the toothbrush in your back pocket, so everyone could see it. Black kids had it sticking out next to their pick, the one with the Black Power fist. Teenagers at the handball courts (they went to Truman) had this leather string sticking out of their pockets. This was a 007, a pocketknife. You pretended you didn't notice, minded your business. You couldn't look soft; you had to have a cool walk. I watched the older guys, their every move.

We took the Bx15 to Onyx on Fordham Road. I was a mama's boy, we were all mama's boys, and my mother only let me go because I was with my older friends. They were black, one was Indian. They were angels, she said, angels. Good kids. When we got to Fordham Road, they said we had each other's backs (you down, Mike?) — that they'll steal these sneakers, even in Co-op. Hide your money in your sock.

I showed up at home room, fewer and fewer white faces, rocking rust on tan Pumas. Yo, where'd you get those? *This was I.S. 181. We weren't little anymore. We wore our navy blue gym shorts under jeans, Lee jeans, creased in the front, and tucked our orange shirts — Northeast Bronx Education Park, it read across the front — into the shorts. Gym was our favorite period, even if there were stories of punks from 180 attacking us in the Truman fieldhouse. They were jealous of us; we had the music program; they gave us instruments to take home. The string orchestra played* 1812 Overture, *the brass band played* The Hustle, *the chorus sang Roberta Flack/Donny Hathaway, "Where Is the Love?" (What happened to those kids? How did life treat them? Are they okay?)*

—

In the fall of 1980, Brooklyn native Jamel Shabazz, just out of the Army, took to the streets and subways, camera in hand, and documented young African Americans and Latinos in Flatbush and Fort Greene, long before liberal white "pioneers" started buying and flipping houses, changing up the neighborhood. (What us natives have been saying for years, since Brooklyn became New Brooklyn, now has a hashtag: #SegregatedBrooklyn.)

The documentary "Jamel Shabazz Street Photographer" — originally released in 2013, but also put out late last year from Oscilloscope, both digitally and as a limited edition DVD with extras — is a revealing portrait of an unheralded New York City visionary. Directed by Charlie Ahearn — himself a visionary, best known for the early hip-hop chronicle *Wild Style* — the likes of KRS-One, Bobbito Garcia, and Fab 5 Freddy offer insights into the photographer's work. (*The Get Down*, the Baz Luhrmann extravaganza soon to be brought to you by Netflix? Did anyone think of including a Shabazz and/or Ahearn as a producer, you wonder?)

If the Manhattan-centric mainstream turned away, or ran away, from these young people, Shabazz did the opposite, what great artists do, and not only came toward them, but immortalized them — looking, as he says, "fly" in Cazal glasses, Kangol hats, sheepskin coats, Lee jeans, adidas and Pumas. Shabazz — part Gordon Parks, part Bruce Davidson, part Bill Cunningham, and even a precursor to the paintings of Kehinde Wiley — gave his subjects, in the words of Fab 5 Freddy, a "nobility" and "blessed them with a royalty." As Jamel's homeboy Tony, a barber, puts it, he was "capturing life in its purest form, man."

All the while, for 20 years, he kept a day job, a difficult one, as a corrections officer. It was only when *The Source* and then *Trace Magazine* published his work in the late 1990s that he got a gallery show — in Paris (not in his hometown) — which was followed by four phenomenal books by powerHouse.

While Shabazz clearly has affection for his childhood and his surroundings, he doesn't romanticize either one. Jamel and Tony remember the friends who didn't make it. They talk about how you had to carry yourself. Shabazz says a similar mien was struck in jail, where he worked, and his neighborhood. "In jail you couldn't appear weak," he says. "You'd get victimized if you didn't walk correct. People could look at you and sense weakness behind your walk. So the way you walked, the way you spoke ... all these things were very relevant growing up."

And while Kirchheimer's subways are all swirls of color, exteriors, Shabazz shows the interiors, where there was "never a dull moment." Another friend, the graffiti artist Sharp, says, "If you didn't want to get robbed, you didn't go back there [to the last subway car]." Like Kirchheimer, Shabazz has an eye for the absurd: "If it concerns you, it concerns us," a local CBS News billboard reads in a subway station, with someone — homeless or worse — lying beneath it. In another photo, a rare subway exterior for Shabazz, the graffiti, circa 1980, reads: "New York City ... where else could I get away with this shit?"

In 1981, Halloween ended — '80, '81. It was when one of the Johnson brothers in my building, the middle son, got jumped and they sprayed Nair on his Afro and his hair fell out. That scared us. He wasn't soft; his father drove a Rolls, I'm serious, with out-of-state plates. (Don't ask questions.) So on Halloween best to stay home. The next morning, the lobby windows were pummeled with eggs, shaving cream, chalk. The cars, too. Thank God ours had been stolen.

That year our social studies teacher called us, his students, the boys, Face. "Yo, Face" or "Ay yo, Face." After school, we listened to the Chief Rocker on BLS and Paco and Rosko on KTU Disco 92, the midday master mix from John "Jellybean" Benitez, maybe Rockers Revenge featuring Donnie Calvin. My boy made mixtapes: "The Glow of Love," Change; "I Hear Music," Unlimited Touch; "Let's Do It," Convertion; "Spank," Jimmy Bo Horne; "I Like What You're Doin' to Me," Young & Company; "Fantastic Voyage," Lakeside; "I'm Ready," Kano. Then Kool & the Gang came out with "Get Down on It."

And what was that song, the one that started "Yo, yo, yo ..."?

Chantal Akerman, the great Belgian filmmaker, took her own life last year. She made a series of exceptional works, most notably *Jeanne Dielman*. *News from Home* — from 1977 — is another extraordinary piece, and one of the great New York films from the era. It's considered experimental though there's nothing austere about it. It's just Akerman, shooting from a car window or the subway while reading letters from her mother, who could be my mother, or yours: worrying, sending care packages, and hoping for a letter in return.

In Akerman's eyes, the city is gentle, if resigned. The subways seem especially placid; if, at first, passengers eye her camera with suspicion, they continue on, minding their business. (I look closely around the frame; maybe I'll see a short, thick man with glasses and a blazer, my father, holding a little boy's hand, running into the subway car or hustling to his office at the Department of Welfare in TriBeCa, before it was "TriBeCa.")

Still, menace, or the perception of menace, lurks: her mother writes, "Just be careful going out alone at night, New York is dangerous"; "I hope your new apartment is affordable and isn't in a dangerous area"; "People here ... say New York is terrible, inhuman. Perhaps they don't really know it and are too quick to judge."

Spoiler alert: Akerman ends the film shooting from a boat (probably the Staten Island Ferry), Manhattan slowly receding into the distance. The scene is painstakingly slow, so beautiful you don't want it to end, but finally it does, as the city fades away, goes gray, as if an apparition. Were we even there?

In 1977 and '78 and the years before and after and into the dreary 1980s, we called Manhattan "the City." If we weren't the city's heart, we were, no, not its soul — that's too easy (even if we did *have soul as Rakim would assure us a few years later). No, maybe we were its spleen, in all senses of the word, something tucked away, off the side — where exactly? — its function unclear, but vital nonetheless. And yeah, a little angry.*

We were white, black more and more, and West Indian and Puerto Rican and Indian and Dominican. We were then what New Brooklyn wishes it could be now. We were middle-middle class, working class, lower-middle class, under class. (Although the Johnsons had a Rolls.) We were inner (city) but outer (borough). And — ha! — all this time, we never knew we were somehow looked through, looked over, looked past, looked down on.

Nothing ever happened to me, not in the '70s, not in the '80s, the subways every day to college, at odd hours. It was the angels, those boys, what they taught me. Or else it was better. Nah, it wasn't better. Except maybe it was. Do you remember?

Last October at The Boiler, a gallery space on North 14th Street in Williamsburg, Aldo Tambellini's transfixing video installation piece *Atlantic in Brooklyn (1971–72)* was on display for the first time in 41 years. Tambellini — a native of upstate New York who migrated down to the city in the 1960s and was part of the thriving experimental film scene — recorded life passing by from his window at the intersection of Atlantic and Flatbush Avenues, now home to an arena constructed by a starchitect, named after an English bank, for an NBA team owned by a Russian billionaire — with a Target, a Starbucks, and a Shake Shack.

There were six chairs in a row in the back of the gallery — and the piece involves six large projections, two each on three walls, repeated on an hour loop; it forced you to swivel this way, that way, the other way to take it all in: a man running; a cop eating; a stray dog; prostitutes milling about in daytime; George McGovern volunteers arguing; church folk strolling; even a few people cycling. There are blacks, whites, Latinos, Asians. One local business offers loans; another donuts, franks, thick shakes. It washes over you.

I've always had a fantasy of walking through the screen of *News from Home* or *Stations of the Elevated* or a Jamel Shabazz photograph. At the gallery, I was pretty much alone — a few people came in, but left soon after — and I just sat there, for over an hour. At one point, I stood up and took a few steps forward. I just stood there.

Postcard HADLEY DAVIS RIERSON

IT'S LIKE A GAME: *Jew, Not Jew?*

Maybe it's because the postcard is from Europe and one of the men, who is rather strapping and maybe even handsome, could have been in The War. Why do I think he could have been in The War? Well, wasn't everyone over there in The War in one way or another?

But it's the other man who could be the Jew. He is small and he has dark hair and it appears that he is skeptical, or disturbed, or perturbed by the man who looks like he could have been in The War.

But the truth is I'd ask the question even if the photograph weren't from Europe and even if the smaller of the two men wasn't dark-haired and possibly perturbed. Unless of course the answer were obvious: like if this were a photograph framed on the wall of a Ralph Lauren store depicting a blond in a boat. Then again, Ralph Lauren — Jew — Lauren a.k.a. Lifshitz, Ralph's original name.

My family's name was Sagalowski, but someone, a great-great-grandfather, had the good sense to change it to Davis. I always liked being a Davis. I thought it made me an incognito Jew. I remember as a child hearing about some horrible hijacking where the terrorists took passengers' passports and, if their name was, say, Goldberg or Goldman or Lifshitz or Sagalowski, shot them in their seats. I would make it off the plane with a name like Davis. I would land safely in Beirut or Karachi.

Now I am no longer a Davis since I married my own non-Jew with relatives who did come from Europe (France, Italy, Germany), and might even have had a distant Nazi cousin or two. (Okay, I'm making that last part up. But it wouldn't surprise me.) I have blond highlights and blond (Jewish) children. And I still play the game.

Freud's Friends in the Countryside

JAY DESHPANDE

Enormous. High up in their wander, gentian
runs into gentian and annual, many for an hour,
in the logic of the hills. Green matching. Wind carry-through.
Sun in its synonym for abundance. And the men
put their well-lit specters on the grass. Who hasn't
been here before? The golden now
and wanting continuance. Or when at an angle
puts his hands up, marring sky to shadow, limit, feels
for a second gorgeously. Weird fruits like that.
At the thought of departure we get an iciness
go clean and boyish down the throat,
the hand, and the hand ever reaching
for girl. Because the world is a she should
stay with me forever. What's ugly is the beautiful
keeps ending, setting us back on ourselves.
Adoration selecting from wilds a bouquet,
leaving the rest. *Here* you think is an out word
and soon as you're dead you're wrong.
Darkness can't ever finish enough of our sentences.
They stayed up there several hours, all the afternoon
parading upon the contemplation,
their face a torque of it. As if it did them better.

< DWYER KILCOLLIN
EMERGENT OBJECT: VESSEL 1, 2014
RESIN AND STONE
13 X 8 X 8", UNIQUE
COURTESY OF THE ARTIST AND M+B GALLERY

The Room

WILL SCHUTT

I found myself in the middle of a room
I barely recognized, a whiteboard
with no lesson on it, walls
wanting for color. The hands of the clock

above the door had been removed.
And my friends had left their seats
in long ordinary rows, in rows

they would never in their lives
have left them in. They must be waiting
in the wings, I thought, cheering me on.

I could sense it. The least I could do
was pick up the marker and draw

what I remembered of the room
when the room was full.

Instead I stood there scrubbing

until there was no board, no boy.

My hands went up, my hands went down.

FAY RAY >
BLUE ORB WITH CACTUS, 2015
GALVANIZED WIRE ROPE, ALUMINUM, EPOXY CLAY, LEAD CRYSTAL
PHOTOGRAPHY BY JOSHUA WHITE/JWPICTURES.COM

ARE WE STILL FABULOUS?

FRANCESCA T. ROYSTER

"Oh you've got green eyes, oh you've got blue eyes, oh you've got gray eyes."
— New Order, "Temptation" (1982)

IN THE EARLY 1980s, Medusa's Juice Bar was a haven for the youth of the neighborhood, even if it wasn't my neighborhood. It was in Lake View, just a few blocks west of the heat of Chicago's Boystown club activity, on Sheffield and School, and it definitely had a queer vibe, even if it didn't yet have the language. Big leather-clad bouncer with bleach-blond hair (and am I remembering right, handcuffs?), house and new wave music: Depeche Mode, Bowie, New Order, Yazoo, Ministry, Frankie Knuckles, a little Prince. Stuff you couldn't hear on the radio. And Grace Jones, of course. The juice part I don't remember because we could only afford water from the bathroom. It wasn't like the teen house music club started by the same owner, Dave Shelton, on 161 West Harrison, which was black and very gay, with the windows steamed up every Friday and Saturday night until it was closed down for being too "wild." What I remember was entering a sea of white, even if it was white cast in purple and blue and black lights. I remember dancing until I sweat, and the hot August Chicago air felt cool again when I stepped outside, until my feet, stuffed into vintage cowboy boots shaped like someone else's feet, cried for mercy. It was fabulous, we were fabulous, if fabulous is to be worthy of the stuff of legend.

Traveling for an hour or more on the Red Line, south to north, we'd start preparing for the evening early with a trip to the Value Village on Kimball. Jorge taught us how to feel the fabrics between our fingers, checking the cotton content, readying our fingertips for linen and silk. Dara's eyes were drawn to the sequins, and chiffon, which she'd cut and snip and resew to be way cooler than even Cyndi Lauper could do. I was always looking for a white linen tuxedo jacket, which I would wear shirtless of course, like Grace Jones, but I never found it. We'd all wear eyeliner. One weekend, I cut all of our hair into the same style, shaved along the left side. After we found our outfits we might go home again, dance and hang out and eat homemade burgers at Dara's house. Her mother was a professional pool and poker player (it was rumored she put Dara through college that way), and was often not around. Or we'd walk down Belmont, linger in Wax Trax! and Second Hand Tunes, grab cheap hotdogs and fries at Devil Dawgs, avoiding the Dunkin' Donuts by the El, which even then seemed a line of danger for us, the desperation of the kids too clear, and the men who waited for the kids desperate, too.

Medusa's was a converted three-flat, and we'd sneak ourselves through a second-floor window via a rusty, rickety fire escape. This was both because we didn't have the admission fee, and because we were only 14 and 15, and the admission age was 16. Sometimes, the bouncer would take pity on us, shake his finger but let us in. Sometimes we were caught and sent back outside, where we'd regroup and try again, or head to the Belden Deli, for coffee and Jell-O or fries or other things that you could get for five dollars or less. We danced together in a circle, keeping an eye out for each other, Jorge and Dara and I. Or we stole away, danced with others, danced like caged go-go girls, danced weaving through the crowd, allowing one another to get lost a little.

Green, blue, gray.

I could listen to this music, this white boy dance music, and reorder my body to its tight muscularity, become new. The funk of my own family, warm and messy and also watchful, was a different kind of sound: the deep feeling of soul — Al Green and Stevie and Whitney and Michael, cut by the no-nonsense of Mavis and Pops Staples. But this music let me think about sex and bodies and even death in a way that felt safer, because it was not-me. In my mind, this was the music of the white gay men I saw walking down Broadway, who captured my curiosity. It was about white men and some women, facing loneliness and their desires, and sometimes their deaths. "For fear your grace should fall / for fear tonight is all," as Bowie said. I could borrow the music, try it on for a while as a mask. This music was both me and not me. This music was not my uncle David, who had disappeared and would return to us decades later, body ravaged and dying, his story cut off from us. His music might be Donny Hathaway or Curtis Mayfield or Luther or even Tupac. The music of black men lost. No one in the family would say that David died from AIDS. But in the tense silence, it was clear.

Brown eyes.

We were black and brown, from Hyde Park and Blue Island and Chatham, "good kids," and our parents knew where we were, more or less. We were in honors classes in our high school, and on the math team and the swim team and the school newspaper and, yes, we loved boys and girls and boygirls. Our bodies matched our names and our voices, and so even though we were black and brown and boygirls, we snuck into the second floor of Medusa's most of the time, the cool-off room where teens and grown people intertwined together, enjoying more than juice, and we were allowed to walk past them and to dance and shine and pose and become our fabulous selves there, and we thought that we were free.

And after that, we moved on. We created new chosen families and had our own children. I drive to work and scan the three-flat where Medusa's once was, the real estate in this neighborhood still unaffordable to me, despite my hard-won degrees. And a few blocks to the east, I see young people like we were, brown and black, staging their fabulousness right there outside on the corners, because they're not let into the bars or allowed to linger at the fancy vintage stores, their backpacks rousing suspicion and hostility. Their names and voices may or may not match their bodies, they may or may not have documentation. Those kids have come from my old neighborhood, or the other neighborhoods to the south and to the west. They may be homeless. They hone their fabulousness under the watchful eyes of the same queers who may have danced with me at Medusa's, who are now the homeowners and the shopkeepers. Aware they are being watched, they laugh with their heads flung back, loud and full.

PAT O'NEILL
1964, 1964
GELATIN SILVER-PRINT
7 X 11.75", UNIQUE
COURTESY CHERRY AND MARTIN, LOS ANGELES; PHOTO: BRIAN FORREST

BEAUTIFUL BEAUTIFUL BEAUTIFUL BEAUTIFUL BOY

BENJAMIN HALE

THE DAKOTA, 1 West 72nd Street. Edward Cabot Clark, head of the Singer Sewing Machine Company, commissioned the building's design from architect Henry Janeway Hardenbergh; construction broke ground in Manhattan's then-undeveloped Upper West Side on October 25, 1880, and was completed four years later. Its layout and floor plan reflect French trends in interior design popular in New York City in the late 19th century, and its decorative exterior shows strong influence of North German Renaissance architecture: high gables, deep roofs, turrets, dormers, terracotta spandrels, panels, niches, and balconies with balustrades. Square-shaped and eight stories high, it fills the city block between 72nd and 73rd on Central Park West, with a porte cochere leading to a courtyard that served as a turnaround for carriages. No two of the building's 65 luxury apartments are alike, as many of them were designed to the specifications of their first occupants, which would have included Edward Cabot Clark himself had he not died two years before construction was completed. Soon after the building was completed it became a point of pride among New York high society to live in the Dakota, and it is still among the most exclusive and expensive addresses in Manhattan. Famous residents have included Leonard Bernstein, Lauren Bacall, Rosemary Clooney, Judy Garland, Lillian Gish, Boris Karloff, Jack Palance, and John Lennon and Yoko Ono.

One hundred years, one month, and 13 days after construction on the Dakota began, Mark David Chapman spent most of December 8, 1980, waiting outside the building's gated south entrance on 72nd Street between Columbus Avenue and Central Park West with a copy of *The Catcher in the Rye*, a Charter Arms .38 Special loaded with hollow-point bullets, and a copy of John Lennon and Yoko Ono's album *Double Fantasy*, which had been released three weeks before. Around midmorning, Chapman met Lennon's housekeeper, who was returning to the building from a walk with Lennon and Ono's only child together, Sean, who was then five years old. Chapman touched the child's hand and said, "Beautiful boy," quoting the song Lennon had written about his son, the final track on the first side of *Double Fantasy*. Around 5:00 p.m., Chapman met Lennon as he and Ono were exiting the building on their way to a recording session. Chapman silently handed him his copy of the album for an autograph, which Lennon obliged, and handed it back, saying, "Is this all you want?" Chapman accepted the autographed album, smiled, and nodded yes. At about 10:50 p.m., Lennon and Ono returned to the Dakota. Ono passed through the gate of the reception area leading into the courtyard, Lennon following a few steps behind her. From directly behind him, Chapman opened fire, discharging the revolver five times in quick succession. The first bullet missed, and the other four landed in Lennon's back.

Derek Fitzsimmons spent most of December 8, 1980, 66 blocks south of the Dakota at the Sheridan Square Playhouse, in dress rehearsal for a production of Charles Ludlam's Ridiculous Theatrical Company's *Love's Tangled Web*, which Ludlam had written and was directing and starring in. Derek was 24 years old. He had graduated from the Fashion Institute of Technology a few years before, and was living with his boyfriend, Tom, in a studio apartment in Forest Hills. He was dressing the actors backstage at the Ridiculous, and performing small onstage roles in Ludlam's productions. Ethyl Eichelberger was in that production. Derek had met Ethyl earlier that year when he was doing wardrobe at the Lucille Lortel Theatre for a production of Caryl Churchill's *Cloud 9*. Ethyl had just moved back to New York from Rhode Island, where he'd been the lead character actor for seven years at Trinity Rep. When she came back to New York, she changed her name from whatever it was before to Ethyl Eichelberger, and got a tattoo of himself as an angel on his back. That tattoo was somehow an important part of Ethyl's becoming Ethyl. Ethyl was only hired to make the wigs for that show at the Lucille, though she had already been in a few of Ludlam's Ridiculous productions, and was beginning to do her solo shows. Derek and Ethyl became friends backstage at the Lucille, and wound up working together often. They both performed in drag, and Ethyl invited Derek to perform in some of her shows. Ethyl was, though only for a brief time, a mentor to Derek.

Six months after John Lennon was assassinated, Derek was at Club S.n.A.F.U. on Sixth Avenue and 21st Street, standing onstage while Ethyl did her Lucrezia Borgia show. Ethyl always beat him to the finish line in the dressing room. Derek's approach to his makeup was delicate and precise. He wanted every false eyelash in place. His lip liner looked machine-etched-on. Derek would lose himself in the mirror, falling into his reflection like Narcissus: spacing out, spending 15 minutes alone perfecting his foundation. Ethyl, 11 years his senior, found this fastidiousness of his silly and endearing — a mark of his youth and relative inexperience. Ethyl's drag aesthetic was decidedly old-fashioned, as far as it could be said that there are conservative schools of the art form. She found it distasteful that some of the younger drag queens seemed to really want to be able to pass for women, with their rubber breasts, worshiping at the style altar of Diana Ross. For Ethyl, the whole thing was supposed to be redolent of the circus, of Weimar Republic cabaret; he wanted a face painted halfway between clown and whore. Ethyl slapped her makeup on in 20 violent minutes: ghost-white foundation, that night, glittering triangles of gold eye shadow with metallic magenta streaks, false lashes like tarantula legs dragged through the black mud of her mascara, red lipstick she stabbed on in three bellicose jerks of the wrist.

Derek was emceeing that night. It was his job to introduce Ethyl, then simply stand back and become a living set piece as Ethyl turned the tiny stage into a lavish spectacle — pure *Satyricon*. Sometimes, before the show, Derek would open with his Rosemary — his first, and admittedly not his most tasteful, drag persona: Rosemary, the Kennedy sister lobotomized by Dr. Walter Freeman and shamefacedly sequestered out of sight, drooling in a rocking chair and gazing vacant-eyed out of some attic window. Rosemary was a combination of a drag performance, a satire on moneyed Cape Cod, and a playground-quality retard act on the maturity level of why-are-you-hitting-yourself, and of course it brought the house down every time.

But on that night, he just did a short stand-up routine before introducing Ethyl. Derek was wearing drag he'd mostly made himself: a tight leather miniskirt and a sequin-spangled silver top with long shimmering tassels swishing down his thighs, sequined pumps that matched the top, chandelier-drop earrings, and his fussily done face of makeup. His hair was his own, long and blond, teased out and gelled up with egg white, scrambled atop his head in an early '60s Brigitte Bardot sort of thing. He was *en costume*, as the obnoxious professional actors he and Ethyl had dressed at the Lucille Theatre would say. After nattering a while at the audience over a jungle of hoots and whistles, he retreated to the side of the stage and very nearly forgot that he himself was part of the show — albeit an ancillary part — and not a spectator, so riveting was Ethyl's Lucrezia.

Derek thought it appropriate that she changed her name to Ethyl, with that spelling, which reminded him of the technical suffix of a chemical: her performances were high-octane spectacles. Ethyl had begun doing these shows because he said he wanted to portray all the great ladies of the stage and history: Jocasta, Clytemnestra, Nefertiti, Medea. His Lucrezia Borgia had something to do with the infamous femme fatale of the Italian Renaissance, but even to call it a character study would be misleading. No two performances were alike, and they always involved half-improvised songs in which she accompanied herself on a big silly accordion that reminded Derek of *The Lawrence Welk Show*. Her repertoire was vast: song, dance, fire-eating, cartwheels. Sometimes he would hire a set painter to paint the backdrop live while he performed, as he did that night.

When the show ended, the DJ put on a Chaka Khan song, "I'm Every Woman," and like a snake shedding its skin, the ambiance of the night slid from performance space to dance party. S.n.A.F.U. was a galaxy of glitter and confetti in a black room that shimmered like outer space, and was as fantastic with alien life: feather boas, leather skirts, wigs, star-shaped sunglasses, boys in ball gowns and girls in pinstripe suits, those slender Audrey Hepburn cigarette holders, the night floating ever higher on champagne and amphetamines and a tremendous lot of cocaine and whatever else was around, strobe lights blitzing, the disco ball throwing spinning multicolored points of light all around. It was nights like these that Derek would later remember as the halcyon days, that flash-in-the-pan golden age of no more than a few years in the late '70s and early '80s between punk and the plague that came, pure Fellini in Technicolor, the sex and fun and wildness without restraint, without shame.

And out of this melee there came a woman. Amid those dazzling spectra of genderfuck and drag there came a woman, dressed in women's clothing, floating like a ghost in Derek's direction — gliding — for she had the primly postured gait of a woman who had once been a little girl made to cross a room with a book balanced on her head. This woman looked as out of place as a Q-tip in a Crayola box at S.n.A.F.U. She was probably about 35 and very Waspy. She seemed to have stepped freshly powdered out of a garden party in the Hamptons. She was short; her impeccably groomed, naturally wavy brown hair was pulled up in a tortoiseshell clip that came up to Derek's midriff (though granted, Derek was five foot 10 and in five-inch heels). She wore a starchy white blouse with puffed sleeves, pleated khaki trousers, tasseled Italian loafers, carried an Yves Saint Laurent handbag. All terribly soigné. Thin white-gold bangles trembled on her slender wrist and caught glints from the disco ball as her bony fingers rose and indicated Derek's outfit, waving without quite pointing up and down his body, and she said, in a feathery voice scarcely audible over Chaka Khan: "I like … *this*."

She came closer, and Derek suddenly felt like he was meeting someone else's mother at a wedding. She held her hand out to him, not vertically, like a salesman about to make his elevator pitch, but horizontally, as if inviting one to kiss it. Derek took the little hand in his — this tiny, perfect hand with tiny, perfectly manicured, lightly blush-colored nails — and did not shake it so much as simply hold it for a moment, soft, cool palms brushing smoothly together. She introduced herself to him as Marianne.

They talked. Her voice was deft and quiet, and her speech grammatical, softly chiming with years of education and centuries of wealth.

"I would very much like for you to come to my home to have your picture taken," she said. Marianne spoke with a hint of that upper-class East Coast accent that was dying out it seemed even then, what used to be called the Transatlantic accent. That voice reminded Derek of Agnes Moorehead from *Bewitched*. (Thank God he hadn't done Rosemary that night.) "I do portraiture, you see, and I am very interested in photographing entertainers."

Entertainers — that was the word she used. Not drag queens, not cross-dressers, but "entertainers." Did she use this gossamer euphemism out of timorousness or politeness? Or some other reason? — some upper-crust noblesse oblige sort of decorousness, which Derek certainly knew about but was not overly familiar with. Derek was the second-to-last of seven children from a blue-collar Irish Catholic family in Poughkeepsie. His had been a childhood of hand-me-downs, burnt steak and baked potatoes, fiercely measured portions at mealtimes. His father died of a heart attack when he was nine, and after that his sisters raised him and his mother wore a green dress and drank herself to sleep on the couch in the afternoons. One of his older sisters was a nun now, and to her, Derek was not an "entertainer," or even a "drag queen," but a sinner, and to his older brothers, he was a freak, a pervert, a queer, a faggot.

A card materialized between his fingers, the apparition vanished, and the night roared into oblivion. The many points of light spun around the room and became a vortex of streaks, smooth horizontal lines of color and whiteness, flashes of fake diamonds and the orange tips of cigarettes. Even here there was a hint of money in the air, or of carelessness, at any rate. Money: the ailment and panacea of the '80s, the real drug we should have said no to. Reagan had told us we had it, and we liked to hear that. Everyone did, including drag queens in squalid basement bars on Sixth Avenue and 21st Street. Derek's memory of that night would fade around three or four in the morning and come back to him when Sunday's dishwater light of about noon slanting in through venetian blinds on a window in his friend Scott's East Village apartment woke him. He was naked and looking directly at Scott's pillow, which he had smeared with the makeup he hadn't removed before bed. Scott was still snoring as Derek picked his things off the floor, and when he made it back to the dingy studio in Forest Hills he shared with Tom, he discovered he had miraculously retained that card. It was a stark beige rectangle of starchy, quality stock, with a name and phone number in crisp gold lettering, and an address at the Beresford on the Upper West Side. With the card in hand, he sank a finger into a plastic hole in the rotary dial of his bedside telephone and fought back an apprehension tightening his throat that surprised him.

The Beresford, 211 Central Park West. With 175 apartments, this preeminent prewar landmark is the largest of four luxury residential buildings on Central Park West designed by the notable Hungarian-American architect Emery Roth, who decorated the massive structure with then-fashionable beaux arts and art deco flourishes of style. The Beresford stands 23-stories tall between 81st and 82nd Streets, with three separate entrances, and three copper-capped towers. The building provides sweeping layouts with ballroom-sized rooms, 10-foot ceilings, wood-burning fireplaces, and private elevator landings. Its mass is relieved by horizontal belt courses in the masonry, and features detailing reminiscent of late Georgian facade work. In the late 18th and early 19th centuries, the advent of steel frames gave rise to skyscrapers, and the citizens of New York, finding themselves living increasingly in shadows, passed the 1916 Zoning Resolution, which outlawed tall buildings from blocking air and light to the streets below; this resulted in The Beresford's expansive setbacks, with 50-foot-wide flagstone terraces overlooking Central Park. Thus, the higher-up apartments on the building's east-facing side are among the most expensive and prestigious residences in New York City.

Derek stood before a doorman in a stately lobby of gold-veined white marble. Derek in jeans and a T-shirt with his long hair knotted loosely in a ponytail and a sparkly purple foil dance bag slung over his shoulder and sagging at his waist, watching the elderly man in his bottle-green uniform with brass buttons murmuring into a desk phone. The doorman's uniform, with its symmetrical and military ceremoniousness, reminded him of a Christmas nutcracker, an impression helped by the deep-creased jowls that made his chin look attached to his face by hidden hinges. Derek had agonized over what to bring. He had figured Marianne would be interested in seeing a few costume changes, so he had brought along as much of the best of his best as would fit in the bag. Lots of makeup, brand-new silver stiletto sandals, the leather miniskirt he'd had on at S.n.A.F.U. the night Marianne had introduced herself to him, jewelry, hairspray, a navy blue top he'd also made himself, which he called his Balenciaga top because of the way he'd cut it — it had ruffles at the bust, and a wonderful way of swinging out in back.

The doorman hung up the phone, smiled, gestured him toward the elevator bank. He rode the elevator with an elevator man dressed in a bottle-green uniform similar to the doorman's. The three walls of the elevator that were not doors were floor-to-ceiling mirrors, creating an illusion of the infinite, Derek's and the elevator man's reflections diminishing into the distance on either side of them. The doors opened onto a small private hallway with a coatrack. There was only one door in it, which was open, and Marianne was standing on its threshold.

Marianne ushered him inside with a courtly "Good afternoon," and in a moment he was standing in the most luxurious interior space he had ever seen. Marianne was at his elbow in an outfit similar to what she had been wearing at S.n.A.F.U. — her hair up, the sleeves of her beige silk blouse rolled up, trousers, and a thin braided leather belt. She would probably have offered to take his coat had he been wearing one. He wasn't, as it was late May: it was humid and overcast outside, a dull, dark day, but warm and sticky, the heavy sort of atmosphere that begs for rain all day and doesn't get it until dinnertime, and then steam rises from the hot streets when the downpour finally splashes them. She didn't have many lights on, which contributed to the melancholy mood in the vast apartment. They stood in a circular foyer; under their feet was a classic compass design of black-and-white marble. She led him in and around, in and around, deeper into the apartment, apologizing all the while for the mess, Derek half-beside and half-behind her, half listening to her and half ogling their surroundings. She was explaining, in her trim, quiet patrician accent, that her husband, Ken, was an architect and that he had designed the apartment's renovation himself, and they were just now moving in and putting on the finishing touches. Derek would remember that thick, sleepy smell of wet paint: everything was freshly done, immaculate, not yet lived in. There were no workmen in the apartment that afternoon, but there were signs here and there of unfinished jobs that someone soon intended to come back to: a paint-speckled ladder, plastic drop cloths, power tools. Unopened cardboard boxes were stacked up in some of the rooms. Most of the rooms had furniture in them, but all the Louis Quatorze tables and chairs seemed to be floating aimlessly in the middle of the parquet and marble floors, awaiting someone's decisions on where they would go. He saw a Chagall painting in a recessed frame leaning against a living room wall, waiting to be hung.

He followed Marianne as she glided across spotless floors that reflected almost as crisply as a mirror. Derek quickly got lost in the space. He'd been in the apartment less than five minutes, and already, if he'd been asked to find his way back to the door he couldn't have done it. He would remember lots of rounded shapes, lots of moldings, lots of warm, pale colors: ecru, apricot, champagne. She led him in and around, in and around: living room, dining room, hallway, another living room, another hallway … and finally, into a bathroom. This bathroom was, it may be said without hyperbole, more spacious by the square foot than Derek and Tom's apartment. Everything blinding white marble: his and hers sinks, toilet, bidet, tub, one of those giant showers you can sit down in, which blasts water at you from the sides as well as from above. The bathroom had an adjoining dressing room — a boudoir, he supposed, with a large vanity table. It was a gorgeous piece — Derek guessed it was something late 19th century and French. Three wide mirrors winged out in triptych, their silvered surfaces faintly veined with age. The surface of the table was, what was it called? — *ormolu* — finely gilt with a coating of high-carat gold.

Marianne gestured toward this museum-quality piece of neoclassical furniture and said, "Please. Do what you do." And then, "Would you like a drink?"

Derek would not remember what he said then, if anything, but Marianne floated out of the room and a while later floated back in again with a Campari on the rocks in a crystal lowball, in which time Derek had unzipped his sparkly purple foil bag and spread his makeup across the vanity table, undressed, and slipped on his pantyhose. He would wear one pair of nude pantyhose to cover the hair on his legs, and then his fancy hose — that day it was stretchy powder-blue fishnet stockings that he rolled on very carefully, as they ripped easily. He began to put on his makeup. The whole apartment was as hushed as a library, the deft clickings of Derek opening and shutting his compacts or popping the cap off a mascara brush the only audible sounds. Derek's own face looked strange to him in the three antique silver mirrors, as if he'd just taken some hallucinogenic whose effect he was feeling but hadn't started tripping yet, and his down-market makeup — all his little drugstore compacts and cheap Brucci lipsticks — looked so absurdly out of place rolling around on Marianne's ormolu vanity table.

So he sat bare-chested in pantyhose and fishnet stockings at the vanity, sipped his glass of Campari, a tinkling red liquid with a spiral of lemon rind in it, and painted his face.

"If you don't mind, I should like to begin," said Marianne.

"Oh? No, I don't mind at all," he must have said.

As he leaned into the mirrors and worked on his face, he began to hear the mechanical snips of an aperture opening and shutting, opening and shutting. He glanced up in the mirror and saw the neat little woman hovering behind him, her face hidden by a big black expensive-looking camera — the most masculine object in the room.

Derek had already been photographed this way many times. All these photographers seemed to love shooting you as you were getting ready, capturing the transition from male to — not female, exactly, but whatever it was on the other side. Drag, for Derek, was not an imitation of the feminine, but was its own third category. Derek had done so many of these in-transition shoots. Every photographer seemed too proud of the idea, confident no one had done it before. Derek had begun to find them tiresome. Every goddamn fashion photographer he had met liked to think of himself as David Hemmings in *Blow-Up*, barking *yes!* and *no!* at you as you did your best Vanessa Redgrave, writhing around on the studio floor. He had begun to feel queasy about it. Something lurid or voyeuristic about how those photographers loved shooting you in half-drag. There is a photograph of Ethyl this way, curled in a bathtub somewhere in the East Village. He's wearing a kind of crenulated tutu, his fishnet stockings — the old-fashioned kind, you can tell by the line on the back of the leg — and an impractical pair of six-inch pumps Derek knew he cherished (and would years later remember him shuffling onto the stage with tight little baby steps, a six-foot-three beanpole under his towering Marie Antoinette wig and polka-band accordion). He doesn't have any trademark wig on, just his own nearly shaved bare head and wild wings of makeup around his eyes, the angel tattoo visible on his bare back, failing to look comfortable in that cramped bathtub, not smiling, but almost sneering. Derek's favorite touches in that photo are the half-visible studio portrait of Ethyl hanging above him in the background, and the drink balanced on the rim of the tub, probably likewise given to him pre-session by the photographer. Every drag queen in the early '80s got photographed in a bathtub at some point.

But with Marianne, he didn't mind. There was very little bluster about this quiet, tiny, middle-aged woman in slacks and slippers who floated around him as he applied his makeup, so quietly he nearly forgot she was there, concentrating, completely losing himself, as he always did, in the mirror. Coral lipstick, electric-blue eye shadow that more or less matched the color of his stockings, rouged cheeks, Cleopatra eyeliner that swept out in elegant strokes of black. When he finished with his face, he strapped on his open-toed silver stiletto sandals and his chandelier-drop earrings. They were real crystal teardrop beads from an old chandelier, mismatched (that was part of their charm), and so heavy they had to be kept on by a wire that curled around the back of the ear. Derek stood to go fishing in his bag for his leather miniskirt, but Marianne lowered her camera and beckoned to him from the doorway.

"If you don't mind, I'd like to photograph you just as you are right now."

Derek shrugged, took his drink, and followed.

The gray afternoon outside the windows suffused the palatial black-and-white rooms in soft pale light. Derek followed Marianne as she looked around the apartment for a good place to shoot him. The spikes of his stilettos made a racket on the parquet floors, echoing solemnly around the half-moved-into apartment.

"I would like it if you would just — just lie down. Right here."

She gestured toward a smooth circular curve in the ivory-colored paneled hallway. It was just a little niche, an architectural hiccup of space between rooms. Derek guessed when the apartment was fully moved into they might put a marble table there with a vase on it or something. The curved wood was what Derek would remember. He'd heard somewhere about the process of making a curved piece of wood like that, how you warp it with steam. There was a round silk carpet on the floor, and he would remember the soft, smooth coolness of it against his back and chest and arms as he lay down on it in a fetal position as Marianne instructed him to do, a position much like Ethyl in that bathtub. The royal blue rug was as soft and silky as a kimono, with a pattern of vines or birds on it. Marianne stood over him, her face behind the camera.

"I love the way your body looks," she said in a near whisper.

Derek writhed around on the floor in slow motion, conforming the contours of his body to the curved white wood.

"Please just move your head," said Marianne.

Obeying her command, Derek quit his full-body squirming and just held still in the pose she wanted, moving his head around. Up, down, side to side, toward her, away from her. In the silence punctuated only by the camera clicks, Derek became acutely conscious of the sound of his own breathing. He looked around at the Escheresque intersection of rooms they were in, at the high ceilings and lighting fixtures, out the windows, which he could see were thinly streaked with the light rain that had broken and was softly pattering the Beresford. He moved his head and looked around at things, and the camera snipped and clacked, followed by the ratcheting sound of Marianne pulling back the lever that advanced the film, followed by a long pause — and then another snip and clack. She went out for a moment and wiggled a stepladder in from another room, climbed it a few steps, and shot downward at Derek as he looked up at her from the floor. The camera snipped and clacked.

“Thank you,” she whispered.

Derek felt a head rush as he finally stood, a tingling of blood, a little sore from lying on the floor. He started off toward what he guessed was the direction of the dressing room, to go get *en costume* in his leather skirt and homemade Balenciaga knockoff. But a feeling made him turn back, to see Marianne putting away her camera equipment, and he realized that “Thank you” meant good-bye. That was all she wanted.

As a child, Derek had mistaken the black spiral in the opening sequence of James Bond movies for a camera aperture rather than a gun barrel. It was not such a far-flung mistake: What is more symbolic of espionage — a gun or a camera? There is a kinship between the two machines. For one, both are “shot.” There is a dialogue between them as symbols. The camera is a hidden eye, whereas a gun is an element of positive space, a protrusion, male. A camera is negative, a hole, a trap. The silhouette of a man saunters into the viewfinder, stops, swivels, and fires directly into the camera, blinding us, the counterspies, the voyeurs, with our own blood.

A couple of weeks later Marianne invited him back to a party at her apartment.

“The apartment is finally done,” that quiet voice said through the honeycomb of holes in the plastic receiver. Derek was lying in bed in the early evening, very high on hashish, carefully dipping Chips Ahoy! in blueberry yogurt and trying to eat them without getting crumbs on his sheets. Derek was in a state of limbo: Tom would be out all night at his bartending job, and Derek was in want of company, but unfortunately he’d already made himself way too high to leave the apartment.

“Ken and I are having a few friends over,” the phone said. “It’s a housewarming of sorts, I suppose.”

“Mn?” he said. “Oh, sure. Why not?”

It could have been a paranoid note from the hash bubbling in his nerves, but he sensed a question lurking behind the invitation, possibly a sexual one. These were days of widespread experimentation; Derek had been on the balcony at Studio 54, and was well versed in three-ways with straight couples. Which he didn’t mind, necessarily, but in any case, as a sort of buffer, he invited Scott along to the party. Tom knew Derek occasionally had sex with Scott. They weren’t “supposed to,” as they were both in relationships with other people, but again, these were days of widespread experimentation. He knew Tom had his own dalliances. Sometimes Derek would feel a wave of guilt, and would say to Tom, “You know, um, I think we really ought to be monogamous.” To which Tom would say, “Yes, I think you’re right about that, yes, absolutely.” And two nights later Derek would be putting on his jacket with his hand on the doorknob, saying, “Oh, I’m just going over to Scott’s to watch *Dallas*.”

(Well, Scott actually did like *Dallas*. Derek didn’t. He never watched *Dallas* and never spent a second of his life wondering who shot J. R.)

Scott and Derek climbed out of the 81st Street subway station and into the early summer night. It was the time of year when everyone is still joyfully surprised that the sun is setting so late in the evening, later every day, meaning only more summer to come. The sky was in what photographers call the golden hour; the faces of the buildings glowing like, well, ormolu, and the shadows of the skyscrapers were long across Central Park. Derek was wearing sandals, a faded black T-shirt with a neckline he’d roughly cut out to bare one shoulder, and red zouave pants tied at the waist with a knotted sash. He loved wearing those pants, especially in warm weather, all that breezy fabric billowing around his legs. Minimal makeup that night — eyeliner, red nail polish, and a touch of glitter on his temple and on his exposed shoulder. He was wearing iridescent dragonfly-wing earrings, and his hair pinned up but loosely falling about his face in a couple of well-placed tendrils that he’d coiled a few times with the curling iron. Altogether his outfit was a little genderfucky, but certainly not drag. He wasn't trying to look like a girl. He never tried to look like a girl. He didn't want to look like a girl, and he didn't want to look like a boy — but simply something other. Not even something in between. Just something else.

Marianne was standing in the marble compass-rose foyer with her husband, Ken, greeting the guests, proper host and hostess. Ken was an attractive man — older than her, about 40, 45 maybe, and imposingly tall. So this was the architect. He wore a genuine smile and didn't seem to talk much, was balding but well built, with eyebrows as white-blond as hoarfrost and kind but arresting blue eyes. He wore khakis and a blue blazer. He had that aura of worldliness architects often have — Derek wouldn't have been surprised to learn Ken had a passion for sailing, or had climbed Mount Kilimanjaro. Marianne was in her usual elegant but restrained attire. Pearls, that night. Derek introduced Scott, shook Ken's large hand, lowered himself to Marianne's face for kisses on cheeks.

Scott was jittery for the bar, and hunting for a drink he quickly disappeared into the fabric of the party, thereafter abandoning Derek for most of the night. Derek would remember emerging into the living room without anyone to lean against socially, Scott already gone and Marianne occupied in the foyer with her husband: that initial lost feeling of walking into a party at which the other guests know one another well, but no one knows you. It wasn't a big party — though granted, one would have to invite quite a lot of people to make that apartment feel crowded. There were maybe 30 people or so, most of them older than Derek, closer to Marianne's and Ken's ages. The apartment had been transformed. If it was impressive when Derek had seen it not quite finished a couple of weeks ago, now it was nothing short of majestic. Everything was in its place: pictures on the wall, furniture all in position. It was complete. The sky had begun to turn purple, and the windows were open to the warm summer night, as were tall French doors that led onto a terrace overlooking the park, and a magnificent breeze blew transparent voile curtains back into the rooms. Somehow a flute of champagne came to be in Derek's hand. Truly, it was a lovely evening. That breeze blew the sheer curtains around, there was laughter here and there, cocktail glasses clinking and chiming, kisses on cheeks, soft conversation. Derek stood by an open window holding his glass of champagne, a line of golden bubbles as thin as a necklace chain ascending to its surface from the stem where he held it, and he looked out at night falling across Central Park from the 23rd floor of the Beresford. *Double Fantasy* was playing, and he would remember that, too. *Double Fantasy* was playing at many cocktail parties in the summer of 1981, but this one was playing at a cocktail party on the Upper West Side, 10 blocks away from where John Lennon had been shot six months before, at a stately, named apartment building similar to the one he was standing in. Lennon sang: "Beautiful, beautiful, beautiful ... beautiful boy." It was a disquieting feeling to be living now in a world in which a Beatle was dead. Derek had guessed Marianne was in her mid-30s, which put the year of her birth sometime in the late '40s, right in the generational crosshairs to be someone for whom the Beatles had truly changed the world. She could have been one of those shrieking teenage girls waiting on the runway at what used to be Idlewild Airport, but had then recently been renamed JFK in the shadow of his assassination (death beatifies). To Derek, the Beatles had never been something new, but something that simply played in the background of his growing up, as the music now played in the background at this party. He had not imagined it would be so soon that he would be listening to this particular dead man's voice. He liked the album. But to listen to that album on the Upper West Side in the summer of 1981 was not just listening to music, but a table rapping, a séance. It was an album of love songs, unexpectedly sweet and guileless ones, without Lennon's usual cast of irony, that drop of venom that made his songwriting so much darker and meaner than McCartney's. And now these love songs had become haunted. The voice of a man who had recently been murdered sang:

"Beautiful, beautiful, beautiful ... beautiful boy." Death beatifies.

It took Derek a little while to realize that many of the people at the party were very ordinary (some of them very large) men who were dressed in women's clothing.

It wasn't drag at all: They were simply wearing women's clothing. They were *en costume* as women who had just come from their jobs at a law firm, or an advertising agency, or perhaps they had picked up their children from school that afternoon. They were wearing conservative, pedestrian outfits: navy blue polyester skirts with little matching jackets, shoulder pads, salmon-pink pantsuits, ruffled silk blouses with bows on them, sensible, low-heeled pumps, pearl chokers, thick black tights. They wore wigs styled in pageboys and bob cuts and whatnot.

Marianne was at his elbow, introducing him to someone. Hands were stuck out to be shaken. He was introduced to a man named Bill in a mousey-brown curly wig. He wore an indigo dress with little white polka dots, and a little gold women's watch on his thick hairy wrist.

"This is my wife, Margaret," said Bill, lightly putting a hand on the back of the woman who stood beside him, similarly attired. As they stood there in that opulent apartment with their drinks, Derek looked around at Bill and Margaret and Marianne, and at the other men around them, at their wigs and skirts and dresses, their makeup. Bill's makeup was of a perfunctory sort, appropriate for the office: lipstick, a little powder and mascara, a hint of rouge on the cheeks. It was poorly applied — he could tell Bill really didn't know anything about the craft of applying makeup. The lipstick spilled over the lines, and his foundation didn't quite match his skin tone. He had probably borrowed his wife's makeup. These men were not trying to be beautiful — they were only trying to be female. But not even that, exactly. There are drag queens who change completely when in drag — an inside-out mental, physical transformation. The voice changes, as do the mannerisms. You instinctively do things such as examine your nails by looking at the back of the hand, with fingers outstretched, instead of looking at the palm with the fingers curled in, the way a man does. Bill was *en costume*, but not *in persona* as a woman. The blue polka-dotted dress he wore had pockets, and the hand that didn't hold his drink he kept casually sunk in one of them as they chatted. Men and women mingled together, couples, friends, some of the men in men's clothing, but most of the men dressed in their pedestrian women's clothing. No one did or said anything that indicated they even noticed anything unusual at all was happening.

He was introduced to another guy, whom he wound up talking to for much of that evening. The man stuck out a hand in an elbow-length black satin glove and said in a deep voice, "Hi, I'm Cathy."

He had a good, strong handshake. He was a tall, squarish man in a houndstooth skirt and a puffy silk blouse the faintly yellowish color of a white key on a very old piano. He wore black hose and white peep-toe slingbacks he must have thought matched the blouse, a quiet string of pearls, and a wig of waxy black hair in a China-chop style, chin length on the sides with straight, tight bangs, like Louise Brooks.

"Beautiful place, isn't it," said Cathy. Derek noticed that Cathy had missed a spot shaving that day; there was a line of tiny moustache hairs just under his nostrils.

"Oh, yes," said Derek. "It's gorgeous."

"Ken did all this himself," said Cathy. "Really dynamite work. Ken is a detail-oriented kind of guy. There's a guy who sweats the details. I can imagine the hell he must have put the contractors through."

It turned out that Cathy was also an architect, a friend of Ken's from "way back," as she put it, "way *way* back."

"This is her virgin voyage," said Cathy. "This little soiree is Ken's way of showing off his work, you know. And it's damned impressive work, I'll say that."

They stood in the apartment and talked about the apartment. Somehow, Cathy fell into taking him on a tour of this apartment neither of them lived in, which Cathy in fact was seeing for the first time and Derek was not. Cathy pointed things out to him, talking about how such and such a detailing element was constructed. Derek glazed over a bit, drinking but trying not to let himself get drunk, finding himself on the receiving end of a lot of prattling straight-guy *explanations* of things. The difference between Greek and Italian marble, things like that. The apartment looked so different from the last time he'd seen it that he couldn't be sure whether or not it was the same place where Marianne had shot him, but it was that same smoothly curved wall that Cathy ran his satin-gloved hand across while explaining how this was done, how they steam the wood to get that curve.

"Damned impressive work," said Cathy, again, for emphasis.

It was fully night, now. People were laughing and smoking on the terrace with the city glittering all around and below them, everyone milling about, waves of people moving through one another. He watched Marianne moving around the rooms, gracious hostess making sure all her guests were enjoying themselves, lightly touching backs and elbows and shoulders, gliding across the radiant parquet and marble floors. She moved so quietly, so elegantly. If there were a pencil attached to her head she could have drawn a straight line across a wall. She reminded Derek of those bar games where you push the stick and the little hockey player moves across the ice. She moved as if she didn't have feet, as if her body rolled along a fixed track in the floor. She was such a serene human being.

Scott had vanished to who knows where, leaving Derek on his own to make it from the Upper West Side all the way back to his shitty apartment in Forest Hills, which would mean spending at least an hour drunk on several subway cars and platforms in his sandals and zouave pants and eyeliner, and it was getting late. It would involve a lot of kissy faces and fag-bashing from gangs of teenagers to be resolutely walked past, through, away from. Not the safest prospect, but he'd done it before, and what else could he do?

So when Cathy offered him a ride, of course he took her up on it. Cathy had mentioned that she lived in, what was it? — Connecticut? Some tony exurb of New York — Greenwich, perhaps — to which he would be driving home over the series of tolled bridges that would bear him back to a gabled Tudor colonial, to wife and children and dog and cat.

It was hardly out of her way, said Cathy; she didn't mind dropping him off at all.

People were collecting their spouses and jackets and purses, slowly filtering toward the door. Cathy, with her blouse and satin gloves and China-chop bangs, excused herself to the restroom, where she was gone for a very long time. Perhaps she was in that same enormous white marble bathroom with the adjoining dressing room, with that 19th-century French ormolu vanity table on which Derek's cheap cosmetics had looked so hilarious a couple of weeks earlier. Derek was talking with the host and hostess on a couch in one of the living rooms as the party wound down around them, waiting for his ride. Ken was sitting in the corner of the couch with a leg crossed, holding a half-drunk Old Fashioned on his knee, looking on with comfort and a gentle aura of proprietorship (Derek by now suspected Ken was wearing lingerie under his clothes) as Marianne perched beside him, depressing the white couch cushions just as much as if she were made of air, Derek nodding along as she talked, trying not to reveal that he had drunk too much. She had the floppy black-and-white contact sheets from their session in her bony little hands, was telling Derek he could come back and have any prints from the shoot he wanted. He would never take her up on the offer. It wasn't because he didn't care, but because he never sufficiently got his shit together for long enough to make that long subway journey back to 81st and Central Park West, and the more time and silence he let pass, the more his embarrassment grew, and the greater became the courage it would have required to pick up the phone and get back in touch with her. Many years later — years after most of his friends had died, and years after he had gotten sober — a friend would call and tell him she thought she saw his picture hanging on a wall in the Bowery Bar. It wasn't a far walk from his apartment in the East Village anyway, and out of curiosity he went in and scanned the walls until he found it. And there he was, nearly 30 years ago, 24, in fishnet stockings and sparkly silver stilettos, makeup, chandelier-drop earrings, and nothing else, lying in a fetal position against the curved white wainscoting on that blue silk rug (you can't tell the color because the picture is in black and white). It only has her name credited on it, and the date: 1981. Derek was one of the ones who would survive the years that followed the shutter that opened and closed on that image. AIDS wasn't even called that yet. It didn't have a name. It was only a dark rumor that most people mistrusted. Ethyl would fire him soon after that picture was taken. Despite his calculated ridiculousness, Ethyl was a very serious performer. He didn't want anyone involved with his act who had problems with drinking or drugs, which soon precluded Derek from performing with him. They lost touch afterward, though he bumped into her occasionally, and sometimes went to her shows. He saw her at Charles Ludlam's funeral in 1987, which he attended in drag. They chatted a while outside the funeral home, Derek having swept aside his netted black veil to smoke a cigarette. Ethyl would die three years later. A suicide, but he had AIDS too. He was on AZT, the only drug available then, and it ravaged his body. He was starving and going blind. Ever the control freak, Ethyl was unwilling to wait for the disease to kill him. Derek heard he had died from Black-Eyed Susan, who had acted with the Ridiculous and still kept in touch with Ethyl. She'd found him in the apartment he was sharing with a roommate in Staten Island. "He slit his wrists like an old Roman in the bath," Susan had said. That phrasing he would remember: "like an old Roman in the bath." She saw Ethyl, emaciated and naked, lying in a bathtub in Staten Island, blood marbling the water, swirling about his body. *Exit Ethyl.* Death beatifies.

Cathy returned from the bathroom, and it took Derek a moment to recognize her. Or him. It was the man beneath the Cathy. He had removed his perfunctory secretary makeup, and his wig, and changed out of his skirt, hose, heels, gloves, pearls, and blouse. He was a tall and blandly handsome man with short blond hair, dressed in a tucked-in yellow Lacoste polo shirt with the little alligator over the heart, khaki shorts, and boating shoes with no socks. He carried an oversized gym bag, which must have contained Cathy. It looked as if he was coming out of the locker room after a tennis match.

They said good-bye to Marianne and Ken then rode the mirrored elevator to the lobby. He was parked on the street, not far from the Beresford. He stuffed the gym bag into the trunk of his gold Buick, and they got in. Ken drove them through the park and over the 59th Street Bridge out to Queens. The night was still warm, and the windows were rolled down. Wind roared in the car, and behind them the blue and yellow lights of Manhattan on a crisp clear night were mirrored upside down in the East River. There wasn't much conversation in that car, in part because it was loud with the windows open, and in part because of something else. At first Derek's aim had been to make it home without getting propositioned, but he sensed an alteration in the mood between them that told him Cathy was completely uninterested in him sexually. They had been chatting quite a bit at the party, and Derek had very lightly flirted with him, as Cathy — but now, they were only a gay man and a straight man who didn't know each other very well in a car together. The man's left arm hung out the window, resting on the side of the door, and his right hand was on the wheel; Derek's hands were in his lap. The space between them had become awkward and stilted. He had learned the man's name by then, but wouldn't remember it: it was something like Chuck, or Charles, or Chase. Chase seemed to fit him, anyway. In striving after things to talk about, they wound up in desultory intervals of conversation discussing the various neighborhoods of Queens, the tennis stadium, the Unisphere in Flushing Meadows. Chase seemed comfortable talking about buildings and landscaping and things like that — those concrete, emotionally neutral subjects that straight men gravitate toward in conversation, the histories and properties of things. Well, a certain kind of thing. There are of course feminine things, such as makeup and chandelier-drop earrings, and there are masculine things, such as buildings and machines. One thing Derek would remember about the 1980s was that there seemed to always be a great deal of discussion about things going on. Stick and carrot, yearning and having, desire and possession.

Derek tried to draw personal information out of him — gently, not wishing to pry, but spurred ahead by frustrated curiosity. What had been bizarre to him was seeing drag that was somehow still inside the box of heterosexual gender relations. This man was not gay. Chase did not want to fuck him. His offer of a ride home was just him being friendly. Derek asked if he was married.

"Uh-huh," said Chase. "The Big Ten's coming up this fall."

"Do you have children?"

"Uh-huh. Two. A girl and boy."

By this time they'd gotten off the highway, and the Buick was idling in front of Derek's squat, cheap apartment building on Jewel Avenue. The odds of ever seeing this man again felt low, and perhaps that was what prompted him at last to just ask him directly.

"What does —" Derek faltered. His hand was on the door handle, and it was late. "What about Cathy? What does your wife think about her?"

"Oh, no. She doesn't know anything about that."

"Oh? She thinks you're —?"

"At a club."

"A club?"

"You know. Athletic club."

"So — you don't identify as gay, or … what?"

Chase smiled and shook his head. He shrugged. The explainer was out of explanations. He didn't seem to like talking about it. He made a sort of gesture toward the back of the car with his head.

"Cathy stays in the trunk. I think it's best that way."

PAT O'NEILL >
UNTITLED (ROSE PARADE), 1966
GELATIN SILVER-PRINT, FRAMED
4.5 X 6.75"
UNIQUE
COURTESY CHERRY AND MARTIN, LOS ANGELES
PHOTO: BRIAN FORREST

Lemon ANIKA FAJARDO

MY MOTHER SAID it was a lemon, but it looked like a red car to me. Lemons were sour and yellow and had interesting nubs on each end. They were filled with seeds that would tumble into the chamomile tea she made for me when I was sick.

The red two-door Datsun F-10 was the first new car my mother ever bought. She doesn't remember the year, but when I look at pictures, I assume it must have been 1978 or '79. It needed new brakes almost as soon as she got it, and there was no stopping them — the car or my mother. She wasn't quite 30, a single parent at a time when the term had barely entered the American vernacular. I was five years old — I rode in the back seat where the triangular windows had their own miniature hand cranks.

I wouldn't see a lemon tree until I was an adult, but pictures of lemons appeared on cans of frozen juice concentrate. My mother dumped the sticky clumps of pulp into a plastic pitcher and mixed them with water. And sometimes we would bring a thermos of lemonade and baggies of crackers to the beach. I watched other children licking Bomb Pops from the concession stand, but I never asked for one because I knew she wouldn't buy it. Afterward, getting in the Datsun all sandy and sweaty, the black vinyl upholstery scalded our legs. At home, unloading the towels and washing the thermos, the backs of her thighs were imprinted with the crosshatch pattern of the seats.

In winter, road salt coated the body of the Datsun F-10, and the doors began to inexplicably rust from the inside out. During one blizzard (those magnificent events that used to happen in Minnesota) my mother drove through clouds of white and then stopped the car. From the cozy back seat I watched a man in a blue uniform get in. I wanted to reach out and touch the icicles that clung to his mustache. After dropping him at the nearest US Post Office, we went home, and my mother made a hot toddy for herself, squeezing lemon juice into a steaming brown mug. Later (or maybe just another time), I squirted honey onto my finger when she wasn't looking.

After the rust (which eventually felled the muffler; a clunk on the highway one day), it was the radiator. The head leaked, I heard my mother explain to a friend. (I studied the front lights and the angular grill, trying to see the head of the car — or even its face — but I couldn't.) Add water, someone told her. So, as if it were an actual tree full of lemons, she began to water her car.

< WALEAD BESHTY
(INSTALLATION VIEW)
MARGINALIA, 2014-2015
THOMAS DANE GALLERY, LONDON.
IMAGE COURTESY THE ARTIST AND THOMAS DANE GALLERY, LONDON

Anti-Elegy

MARCI CALABRETTA CANCIO-BELLO

For my mother, who twisted her hair
every day into a knot held by
a wooden pin knobbed with jade.

For my father, who combed our island
looking for the most deformed trees,
measured water into the shallow bases
of his bonsai sprigs, waited years
for me to grow into my long fingers.

For Grandmother, whose skin smelled
of seaweed, who asked me always to eat
the sweet abalone porridge with her.

For what the sea gives up and asks
to be returned, for the tide.

For the water deer, who moved and mated
the night my brother first wept, as though
offering their own children to his grief.

For my brother, who did not die
no matter how many times we killed him.

– For we are not our own.

Brother Returns as Dragonfly

MARCI CALABRETTA CANCIO-BELLO

Sunlight drips from fists
of clouds, bronzes white sand.
Arms hoary with coral,
the sea gathers each minnow
back into her skirt. All day
she has been prying secrets
from the mouths of clams,
catching at my brother's legs.
He comes to me every night,
sits on my stomach, digs
his fingers through my rib cage
for the bivalves of breath.
He follows me into the bathroom,
pisses seawater into my sink.
We kneel on the tile floor, folding
the shadows of our fingers
into pigs and ibis, spotted fawns.
Birthmark on his shoulder
shaped like the shoreline, dark
as a lung, fists full of water.
Even as the sun shrugs out
of its daily sweater of stars
too early, he unfurls his fists,
and says: forgiveness
is not a star, it is a dragonfly.

A FIDELITY, AN INDIGNATION — A TRIBUTE TO BENEDICT ANDERSON (1936 – 2015)

GOENAWAN MOHAMAD

TRANSLATED FROM THE INDONESIAN
BY JENNIFER LINDSAY AND THE AUTHOR

ON DECEMBER 13, 2015, Benedict Anderson died a beautiful death. He spent his last hours in Batu, East Java, a scenic part of Indonesia to which he was especially attached. His remains were cremated 100 kilometers away to the north, in Surabaya, the iconic city of the Indonesian Revolution — a historic event Anderson called in one of his famous books a *pemuda* revolution. And it was always to the *pemuda* — young people — that Anderson showed his affection, as Perry Anderson, his brother, said in a simple funeral ceremony inside the Surabaya morgue.

Not surprisingly, most of the mourners who later carried his ashes and spread them over the Java Sea were young. The last lecture he gave at the University of Indonesia, three days before his death, was attended by hundreds of students, activists, and public intellectuals, all under 40 years old.

Indonesia was, as many would say, Anderson's adopted country. To most Indonesians who were his friends, including myself, he was never a foreigner. I called him "Mas Ben," and he called me "Mas Goen" — *mas* being a Javanese word implying respect and intimacy. But it was not culture, history, or geography that made Indonesia Mas Ben's focus of study and attention. In the beginning it was a "political awakening" that had little to do with Southeast Asia.

It happened in Cambridge, when Anderson was 20. As he described it:

> My political awakening came [...] in 1956, when I was a 20-year-old student at Cambridge University. In that year Britain, France, and Israel declared war on the nationalist military regime in Egypt. Walking back to my room, I noticed a small group of slender Indian and Sri Lankan students passionately orating against the war and Prime Minister Eden's barefaced lies. Listening to them out of idle curiosity, I was stunned when a phalanx of large-bodied, enraged "Aryans" came to beat up the brown-skinned orators. Feebly trying to intervene, I found my spectacles torn off my nose and trampled into fragments on the grass. I had never been so angry in my life.

DWYER KILCOLLIN
BANQUET, CONFERENCE, 2015
RESIN, FELDSPAR, CALCIUM CARBONATE, QUARTZ, SILICA, GLASS
43 X 98 X 71"
UNIQUE
COURTESY OF THE ARTIST AND M+B GALLERY

That anger was Anderson's "moment," as he put it. It led him to go into "the agony of decolonisation" in the former colonies in Asia and Africa — and most probably influenced his decision to go to Cornell University in the United States. The brilliant graduate of the Faculty of Classics of Cambridge University decided to change his course; he wanted to study Indonesia.

At the time, he said in early 1958, "right-wing elements with CIA support" in Indonesia had almost succeeded in opposing a "left-wing" president, Sukarno.

Anderson was, of course, referring to rebellions in Sumatra and Sulawesi, triggered by widespread grievances among people in the major islands outside Java but mostly dictated by anticommunist army officers who saw that Indonesia, under President Sukarno, was drifting to the left. To be sure, the story of the CIA-supported rebellions was more complicated than the way the young Anderson surmised it, but what was important was his impulsion. Anderson, who had studied, albeit briefly, under the Marxist historian Eric Hobsbawm, wanted to confirm and conceptualize the anger he had felt that day on the Cambridge University campus: an anticolonialist outrage, an indignation at any scheme of exploitation and inequality.

In 1962, Anderson came to Jakarta. For the next two years he did research, gathered data, and lived "happily in chaotic Indonesia."

I met him for the first time on a Jakarta roadside in 1963. He was 27, and I was 22. Mas Ben was sitting next to Onghokham, my friend at the University of Indonesia who had become Ben's best friend in his early days in Indonesia; both were busily eating durian, a local fruit with a strong smell, which ordinary foreigners love to avoid.

In Indonesia, and about Indonesia, Anderson was obviously enthralled. He immediately made friends with students, intellectuals, and political activists (mostly of the left-wing and *abangan*, or "secular," persuasion), and traveled deep into the central and eastern parts of Java. His regular companion was of course Onghokham, who was then a student in the history department at the University of Indonesia. With errant, eccentric, and indefatigable Ong as his guide, Ben was "dragged into" (as he put it) a fascination with "temples, gamelan, wayang, village performances, stories, manners, *batik* [...]."

He became intimate with all these things, as he continuously explored territories far under the usual radar of other scholars, particularly social scientists — hence his original way of seeing and his uncommon list of findings. His essay "The Idea of Power in Javanese Culture," for instance, was an effort to offer "a systematic exposition of traditional Javanese conceptions about politics" that previous writers had not recognized. His intention, Anderson said, was "to describe the picture of social and political life seen through traditional Javanese lenses, and to draw explicit contrasts with the picture seen through the lenses of modern social science." By using "traditional Javanese lenses," Anderson claimed to discover that in "the Javanese theory of politics" the conception of power differed "radically" from the concept of power in "the West since the Middle Ages." As a result, there were "contrasting views of the workings of politics and history."

This, of course, was an extremely interesting observation and a bold step into the development of the so-called scientific phenomenology of culture, which Clifford Geertz initiated in his analysis of Balinese cultural tradition.

However, from the outset, the proposition was problematic. Radically different things may be outside the logic of comparison, and as Anderson admitted, he could not find a generic concept of "power" that covered both the "Javanese" and the "Western" notions of it. The Javanese, according to him, had no equivalent word for the concept.

The dissimilarity was also a contrast. In Western political theory, Anderson suggested, power was abstract, while to the Javanese, it was concrete. It was to him "that intangible, mysterious, and divine energy." It was the very energy that animated the universe.

The way Anderson described it — and it won an arguably widespread following — made political behaviors of the Javanese enigmatic, intriguing, or sometimes baffling to political analysts from around the world. But one can accuse Anderson's essay, published in 1972, of perpetuating the unfortunate legacy of the colonial perspective in anthropology; it has a trace of what Johannes Fabian famously calls "a denial of coevalness." Its "essentialist" bias — describing things Javanese as if they were not shaped and transformed by history — is another target of criticism.

The basic problem is that Anderson did not clarify what he meant by "Java." Growing up in the Indonesian province called Central Java, I was, and still am, very sensitive to the intricacy of being "Javanese." I spent my childhood in the northern part of the province, close to the sea, where people did not speak the language accredited as "Javanese" by government-run institutions. Privately we resented this imposition; my father, who was a clandestine member of the first generation of the Indonesian Communist Party, was particularly resistant to the "Javanese" hierarchy-based vocabulary and manner of speaking. Although finally I acquired a good degree of "Javanese" proficiency, I was never sure how possible it was to become truly "Javanese."

In the colonial management of the population, which is blindly perpetuated to this day, "Java" was a demographic and cultural identity constructed by ignoring the diversity of those who live between the borders of West Java and East Java, and by denying their endemic conflicts and tussles for hegemony.

Besides, the meaning that invokes "a unique amalgam" (as Anderson put it) called "Java" is actually the representation of *cara Jawi*, or "Javanese manners," which, as John Pemberton showed in *On the Subject of "Java"*, were formulated only in the mid-19th century. *Cara Jawi* were implemented when the central Javanese kingdoms were threatened by Dutch aggressive intrusion into the territory, and as a consequence the palaces, in this case the Surakarta palace, felt the need to fortify themselves by building rituals, which to outsiders, to the Dutch, were virtually impermeable.

Had Ben Anderson seen "Java" as a word impregnated by history, I think he would not have written "The Idea of Power."

~

But two things later freed Anderson from his early fascination with the perpetual amalgam called "Java."

The first was the savagery of October 1965, when thousands of people marked as communists were slaughtered — the ferocity of which traumatized Anderson's dear friend Onghokham, who later, in drink, tried to obliterate his nightmare of the rows of bloodied bodies he had seen beside the road in East Java. To Anderson, hearing of the mass slaughter in the country that had so enchanted him was like being told his own brother was a murderer.

The massacre was often described as a reprisal against the killing of six anticommunist army generals (one of them was the powerful chief of staff). The army and other political parties, who had always felt threatened by the increasing power of the PKI — which was then the world's third-largest communist party — immediately believed that the Party had concocted the plot and steered a group of younger officers to act against their superiors. The army propagated the view that the "movement" was a PKI coup d'état, and a murderous one at that. The fear of a possible communist takeover spread. In no time, various anticommunist groups, Muslim and others who saw the PKI as a real threat to their survival, started the carnage in different parts of the archipelago, aided by the army.

Shocked and outraged by the brutality, Anderson, together with Ruth McVey and Frederick Bunnell, all from Cornell University's network of academics, quickly responded by writing "A Preliminary Analysis of the October 1, 1965 Coup in Indonesia."

Better known as the "Cornell Paper," it was a powerful piece. Many Indonesians who lived in Indonesia, especially in Central and East Java, found the paper, written in a place thousands of miles away from the site of the convoluted violence, presumptuous. They thought the intricacy of the issue did not warrant any instant judgment, especially by people whose lives were not at stake. But I found the paper to be quite a perceptive analysis, with a well-researched description of the endemic conflicts within the Indonesian Army. It also correctly refuted the prevailing allegation that the "October 1 Movement" was a coup d'état, since the plotters indicated no plan to topple the head of state, Sukarno. The man who presided over Indonesia's left-leaning "Guided Democracy" was never an ally of the anticommunists.

The Cornell Paper theorized that the PKI had no part in the plot against the murdered generals. Instead, the party was a victim of this internal army conflict; the authors claimed the PKI was entangled before it knew what was happening.

Admittedly, the paper, a "preliminary analysis," was based on preliminary data. Further findings confirmed, contrary to the paper's assumption, that the PKI chairman, Aidit — together with his closest confidants — was deeply involved with the plot. From a standard Marxist-Leninist perspective, his was an unorthodox act; in fact, after the debacle, many PKI cadres privately blamed Aidit for the massive destruction it brought to the party. But there was another plausible interpretation of the kidnapping and murder of the generals: it was a way to purge "counterrevolutionary" top brass who for many years had blocked the PKI's further step to power. Aidit might have believed that the only way to complete the PKI's ascendency in the contentious politics of the "National Front" — which was a mandatory, albeit spurious, alliance between existing political parties against "neocolonialism" — was to mobilize pro-communist officers to get rid of the generals. Strong as it was, the PKI's position in the Front was precariously dependent on its ally and protector, Sukarno — and in 1965, the exalted "Great Leader of the Revolution" was reportedly in ill health.

Whatever the actual game plan was, it badly miscarried. After liquidating the commanding officers of the army, the plotters occupied the national radio station and announced their loyalty to Sukarno, and yet they failed to take control of Jakarta, the capital city. Not a single mass rally came to their support. There was no Sukarno endorsement. And despite the setback to the army, its headquarters remained far beyond the plotters' reach. When some hours later the army, led by a rather obscure general named Suharto, struck back, the "revolutionary" troops put up the white flag without much resistance.

Suharto triumphed. He also gained something else: he and his lieutenants found an excuse to annihilate the PKI. Suharto intensified the massacre and the witch hunt. In his hands, in the grip of his repressive regime, power was no longer the "intangible, mysterious, and divine energy" as Anderson described it. Instead, it was equal to sovereignty of the New Order kind; its political body decided who belonged to "bare life," as Agamben terms it, and who did not.

—

The second influence that changed Anderson's perspective was his younger brother. Perry Anderson, historian, former editor of the *New Left Review* (Ben half-jokingly called him his older brother intellectually), convinced him that "Indonesians were, after all, part of the human species, and could not possibly be incomparable and unique."

In other words, like everybody else, Indonesians cannot be ahistorical. One has to restore history and politics into the discourse. Anderson, banned from coming to Indonesia for 27 years by the Suharto regime because of his role in the production of the Cornell Paper, had the opportunity to take distance from the country and embark on studies of comparative politics — and he did it brilliantly. Hence his famous work *Imagined Communities*; it was an attempt, as he put it, to combine "a kind of historical materialism" with what later came to be called "discourse analysis."

With this Marxist perspective ("Marxist modernism married to post-modernism *avant la lettre*," Anderson said) he discussed nationalism in various distant places and in differing chronologies.

—

What people often get wrong when they read *Imagined Communities* is the universal element in those various nationalisms. As I see it, this universal element is neither the global use of technology and the capital of "print capitalism," nor the failed universality of religions, but the dialectics of servitude. Colonialism produces the indignation of the colonialized. Sukarno would use the metaphor of the rebellion of the worm — even though merely a worm — when trodden upon.

Without widespread protest against colonial dominance, "print capitalism" would have no effect. There has to be a good degree of, to use Rancière's words, "political subjectivation" — namely the ability to produce the "polemic" that expresses the contradiction between the police order (*la police*) and politics (*la politique*). And "politics" here means actions that rock that order, defying "the distribution of the sensible," so that the unrecognized become present, the voiceless speak, the marginalized emerge, and those kept in the dark appear.

To me the most apt description of *Imagined Communities* is Gopal Balakrishnan's in *Mapping the Nation*: "Anderson's book is a reminder that, at its best, imagined nationhood in all its crudity has been the entry ticket for the wretched of the earth into world history."

—

As a boy, Ben Anderson loved to read Sherlock Holmes stories. He always remembered the detective's message: when studying a case, it is not enough to analyze the evidence, "a detective has to notice what is absent, invisible."

Maybe this is why Anderson tended to shine light on the invisible, and bring out the absent. Whereas before him people wrote the history of nationalism from ideas and wars between powers, Anderson saw it (in a historical materialist fashion) in sheets of newspaper, in the relationship between printing, market, capital, and language, or in the census, museums, maps, and tombs to unknown heroes.

Anderson himself tended to be attracted to the scattered social practices of the streets — things virtually invisible from above because they are neither glorious nor glorified.

I happen to know that from the late 1970s, he was close to Pipit Rochijat, an Indonesian student activist in Germany who became well known in the 1980s as the creator of sharp comic-strip parodies about the Suharto regime — which resulted in him being banned from returning to his homeland. Pipit chose to be outside any line. A devil in his thinking, someone who loved to mock and who wrote in an eccentric kind of Indonesian, Ben found this young, spirited, and creative émigré in Berlin immediately attractive. Anderson's letters to him (Pipit permitted me to read them) showed another side to the author of *Imagined Communities*: not the scholar famous for his impressive scope and fascinating prose, but Ben, who, with his ever-youthful insolence, loved to joke with unconventional, rude, sarcastic, and "inappropriate" talk.

In snappy Indonesian, he flawlessly adopted Jakarta street slang, Javanese dirty words, and irreverent remarks on death and state dignitaries. In an unpublished piece that he also sent to Pipit, he contrasted the *Taman Pahlawan*, or Heroes' Cemeteries, full of names of the great and high-ranking, with the graveyards of people he called "fighters" (*djago*) — warriors without hierarchy. "It's hard to slip their bodies into the Heroes' Cemeteries where the immigration officers are so vigilant," Ben wrote in acerbic Indonesian.

> You never see their names on street signs. But while Heroes' Cemeteries are sites of pilgrimage only for official groups and at specific times determined by the authorities, these other 'fighters' who are buried in neighborhood graveyards live on in all kinds of collective memory, in poetry and in folk theater.

We know where Ben's heart lay.

Consciously or not, there is a constant thread between the mocking language ridiculing state-appointed heroes and Anderson's indignation on the Cambridge campus in 1956. Directly or not, there is continuity between siding with the silenced and the ignored, and *la politique*, action that rocks the order that institutionalizes that dividing.

To be sure, the nation as an "imagined community" can indeed grow into a sovereignty that is discriminatory and repressive. But the process of imagining in the history of nationalism that Anderson proposed is part of the dialectics of history, always occurring with outbursts of antagonism: revolt against the status quo — sometimes on a godless, iconoclastic premise, other times on religion-based sentiment.

Failing to discern the radical ethos of politics in the process of the nation's becoming — as in the case of the Vietnamese and Indonesian revolutions — means one will also fail to recognize the rupture and the transformation that nationalism produces. In his study of nationalism in Southeast Asia, *Imperial Alchemy*, Anthony Reid describes it, in a very apt metaphor, as the work of "the revolutionary alchemist" who transmutes "the base metal of empire" into "the gold of nationhood." To surmise as Partha Chatterjee does, in his criticism of Anderson's theses, that "even our imaginations must remain forever colonised" is to miss the transformative force of a nationalist revolution.

Between the lines of Anderson's leftist theses is an appreciation of that force — and his generally positive view of nationalism. "I am probably the only one writing about nationalism who doesn't think it ugly," he said in 2005, in an interview at the international literary festival in Stavanger, Norway. "I like its Utopian elements."

Anderson acknowledged that nationalism has a strange magic that gives a sense of "moral grandeur" to self-denial. His *Java in a Time of Revolution: Occupation and Resistance, 1944-1946* gives a sympathetic description of the way Indonesian "popular nationalism," especially among the young, the *pemuda*, grew. In the years preceding Indonesia's declaration of independence, the *pemuda*, sensing "an impending historical moment," prepared themselves to practice the idea of "self-sacrifice, austerity, fraternity, and heroism."

Interestingly, it was the young who believed in the power of the *semangat* (spirit) of revolt more than anything else, who were the icon of Anderson's narrative. No doubt, his notion of emancipation implied an anarchic imagination. *Under Three Flags*, the Indonesian translation of which was published just a few days before he died, is actually a statement of "anarchism." More precisely, it is an "anarchism without adjectives," to use the formula of Fernando Tarrida del Mármol, the leftist figure whose story Anderson relates in such a fascinating way.

At the end of his book, Anderson tells how at a meeting of activists in Manila he read to the audience an unsigned pamphlet he had come across: "Organize Without Leaders!"

And he loved it.

This is where Ben Anderson has no parallel. A Marxist who hardly quoted Marx, an anarchist without adjective, a progressive scholar who never wore labels. He was exceptional not only in his various theses that made us think, but also in his fidelity to the indignation of his young years, from that day on the campus of Cambridge.

Tooth MARY OTIS

THE CAMPUS OF the Findley Academy entraps decades worth of girls' secrets — girls who leap across the quad with big, unsorted dreams of the future rolling around in their brains, girls who cry behind bushes and pillars that fail to hide them, and girl after girl after girl who stands before the gaping mouth of her coffin-like locker stuffed with schoolbooks, love letters, and messages to self, single words of hope and despair that read *Now* or *Never*, not to mention the girls who scrawl on the inside of their locker doors cryptic and nasty fuck you symbols amid the detritus of make-up, packs of Marlboro Lights, the good-luck voodoo doll lying on the tiny mattress of a long-lost sandwich, and jumbo-size spray cans of knockoff designer perfumes like the Opium imposter Ninja and an Obsession fake called Confess, which they apply on the sly, inexpertly, like bug spray. Too much! And this is the thing about these girls they're too much, even the quiet ones like Calla Fortuni, who keeps an extracted tooth, a fang, really, in a velvet box inside her locker, each of them serving out their sentence, roaming the halls of the Findley Academy loaded up with so much emotion they might as well have explosives strapped to their backs. Girls are dangerous, and girls are good, and girls will never be this way again.

< ALIKA COOPER
STRIP TEASE, 2016
VINYL PAINT AND FABRIC ON WOOD PANEL
14 X 11".

Courtship Displays of the Blue-Footed Booby

SARAH LINDSAY

for RLB

His strut was nothing special:
waving the feet high, splatting them down.
His flight display delineated
a modest territory. Then came
the presents of nest material. First,
a thing like a stone with ravines for secrets.
A peach pit, he told me – he'd heard its fruit
was sweet and soft, with skin
that blushed like a sunset. Second,
a tuft of long grass bent at one end.
Trodden perhaps by iguanas, he said,
or pressed beneath the deliberate foot
of a giant tortoise with shining eyes,
hauling sandward her unlaid eggs.
Then again, he said, a human
might have stepped on the grass,
as they step on so much, or crushed it
under a box, and we could spend years
on the things they put in boxes,
but he turned to his third gift instead, a posy
of feathers tweaked from his breast.
We threw back our heads: He gave the high whistle,
I made my low reply. I bowed
to my new possessions, swaddled in stories.
His feet were heavenly blue.

A Mostly Canceled Universe

SARAH LINDSAY

Maybe monotony ruled
the first one-trillionth of a second,
but for all the time we know about,
the universe has been a duel
between matter and antimatter –
each to the other Devourer, Cain,
Tiamat the Dragon, evil twin.
Where there are two there's competition,
and in the contest for "God likes me best,"
matter comes out ahead:
It's fifty point five percent of everything.

But what would we or anything be
without the enemy, always doing
its forty-nine point five percent best
to cancel out matter?
Conflict made room for darkness
in a cosmos full of burning,
room for star-suds to drift into clumps of foam,
room to open spiral arms,
for infant planets to spin with their sisters,
for air to roll from a cello's body
or spool from a flute,

for wind to advance its chess-clouds, bearing
minuscule, weightless spiders and snails
that ride to new places
and come down in rain.
Without the opposing almost-half,
could anything orbit, or float, or swell?
A single muffled note might sound,
a vibration slowed by the cold
of close-packed atoms nearing stillness,
a wave with one peak at this side of the universe,
one at the other, far too low
for the whorled ears of galaxies,
if they had formed, to hear.

Bonne Année
FRANCAISE
POSTES

Postcard KATIE WECH

SUCH A PRETTY CARD. They're holding hands. Was that their idea? Or are they doing the bidding of the off-camera dresser (and apparent lover of little sailor ties)? I look at those calm little faces, and suddenly the older one, the big sister, is scowling at me — I'm caught in a tractor beam of wrath — she's my four-year-old girl, the boss, the life force, the hellion who (I've always said) has always been this way. Vigorous, physical. All right, all right — aggressive. Which brings me to the boy. The little one. He seems sweet like my little one is sweet, except were it my boy in the photo, having been recently clobbered by his sister, he wouldn't be smiling.

I don't understand the violence. Her penchant for it, his seeming desire to provoke it. Two and a half years old, his entire life, he's been subject to her clocking him, pushing him — one of my earliest memories of the two of them together is bringing him home and putting him in a swing, this tiny fragile bundle, *just like a pork loin* I remember saying when he landed on my chest after I delivered him. Ten seconds later we caught her dragging him out of the swing, his soft head just seconds from cracking onto the hardwood. I don't think she dislikes him. I think she loves him with a fire that could incinerate him. I think she thinks he's *hers*, and when he moves of his own mind it both surprises and infuriates her. She is consumed then, her only recourse becomes physical. You see it build up in her, the dam walls stretch and creak and finally burst, 10 times a day, her feelings are a tidal wave, and we all run for a boat, a branch, higher ground. Except him. He bobs along, a buoy, complicit in this latest tempest whether he'd admit it or not. This is their discourse, their relationship. To some extent, maybe it's not my business to understand how or why it is this way, why he draws out this behavior, why she is so quick to retaliate. But beneath his piteous cries as she chases him, sits on him, bonks him (with a Barbie car), I can hear it, it's not my imagination, and it's not misery — I know it, they know it — it's delight.

And it wouldn't make a pretty card.

WHY CAN'T YOU BE SWEET?

AMANDA FORTINI

She remembered them all in an embarrassing blur: the pretty, delicate drug addict, the masochistic Chinese boy, the pretentious Italian journalist, the married professor, the pompous law student, the half-crazy club owner who almost strangled her one night with his belt. The guy she met and screwed in the rest room of some tiny East Village bar, the one who later involved her in an exhausting ménage à trois with his Italian girlfriend.
— Mary Gaitskill, "Connection," *Bad Behavior*

Well Rhonda had a house in Venice,
Lived on brown rice and cocaine.
Patty had a house in Houston,
Shot cough syrup in her veins.
Linda thought her life was empty,
Filled it up with alcohol.
Katherine was much too pretty,
She didn't do that shit at all.
— The Nails, "88 Lines About 44 Women."

My desert-island, all-time, top five most memorable split-ups,
in chronological order:
Allison Ashworth
Penny Hardwick
Jackie Allen
Charlie Nicholson
Sarah Kendrew
Those were the ones that really hurt.
— Nick Hornby, *High Fidelity*

1.

"LEO WAS FROM a long time ago, the first one I ever saw nude," begins "Lust," the title story of Susan Minot's 1989 collection. "In the spring before the Hellmans filled their pool, we'd go down there in the deep end, with baby oil, and like that." The story, told mostly in the first person, breezes through the narrator's dalliances with various boys while a teenager at boarding school. "Tim pinned me to a tree, the woods light brown and dark brown, a white house half hidden with the lights already on," Minot writes. And then, as swiftly and as lyrically as she introduced us to these boys, she recounts the wounds inflicted by her entanglements with them: "After sex, you curl up like a shrimp, something deep inside you ruined, slammed in a place that sickens at slamming, and slowly you fill up with an overwhelming sadness, an elusive gaping worry."

"Lust" moves in and out of the second person, the you, you, you enlisting the reader in the story and highlighting the universality of such amorous tales. If you've had sex, you have stories to tell about the people you've had sex with. I got to thinking about this the other night, as I lay on the couch talking by phone with Catherine, whom I've known since college. She was remembering the guy who told her he could only sleep on high-thread-count sheets. That reminded me of a man I knew, an investment banker eight years my senior, who bought me 600-thread-count Egyptian cotton sheets the weekend I moved to New York — I was sick with the flu and sleeping on a bare mattress. He'd visited me at college the previous fall, seen the dark dorm room where I was writing, and shipped me a pair of Pottery Barn lamps. We slept together off and on for a year, and our affair might have lasted longer were it not for the oppressive onslaught of expensive gifts and the fact that, when he inscribed a book to me, he misspelled their "thier." When I think of him now, the presents and the inscription, along with a handful of stray details — his syrupy Southern drawl, his persnickety habit of straightening his place settings at restaurants and correcting my slouchy posture — are almost all I remember about him.

"Mike was in the Navy, though I cannot see the sea in him. I cannot see ocean," opens Louise Wareham Leonard's slim autobiographical novel *52 Men*. Narrated by her fictional alter ego, Elise McKnight, the book consists of 52 formative episodes with various men, and is set mostly in and around New York City. "We walk in the local park. It is autumn and cold and the leaves are rust-colored, spiky," the passage continues. "Mike is good-looking with black hair and blue eyes. He is gentle and very quiet. When he calls me, a week later, I have a hard time placing him. '*Mike*,' he keeps saying, '*Mike*, *Mike* from the *park*.'" In this flat, affectless prose, which oscillates between austerely effective and irritatingly mannered, Leonard-as-McKnight shares her personal collection of the sort of romantic memories we all have: the stories, anecdotes, and small details of those we've crushed on, obsessed over, dated, fucked, pined for, been hurt by, left. These are not stories of love, of deep affection that takes root and blossoms into engagement or marriage. These are stories of brief encounters, some of them sexual, a few genuinely traumatic — of the people who flicker in and out of our lives, who flare brightly for a moment and then are gone.

It is a conceit so simple and ingenious that you wish you had thought of it yourself: 52 men — a few boys, many man-boys; 52 short fictional vignettes that evoke them. (There's also an extended 53rd episode, but I'll get to that.) There's Eddie, a 28-year-old phone company salesman, who lives in a one-bedroom apartment off Columbus Circle. "He has a stack of videos and books about the penal system, and *The Hitchhiker's Guide to the Galaxy*," Leonard writes. Elise is involved with a married man, so she and Eddie smoke pot together, keep things platonic. When her married lover returns to his wife, Elise leaves the country, never to see Eddie again. There's Peter, a small, fast seven-year-old, who merits only four lines. He gives her what she believes is a love note; inside, she finds "the crushed body of a black fly, wings broken, round oily hot eyes." There's Alain from Queens, who works in freight, owns six vintage cars, and lives in a 20-room house on the Brooklyn Heights Promenade. He "is broken, and very gentle," Elise tells us. "*You have saved me*," he writes to her, "*from the jaws of despair*." Perhaps in gratitude, he buys her stuff: a leather blazer, Frederic Fekkai haircuts, Cole Haan shoes, a tank watch from Coach. "When he has known me longer," Elise says, drily parroting him, "He will buy me a better watch." So that's three — there are 49 more.

Leonard doesn't develop her characters so much as conjure them with quick, precise strokes. Her impressionistic portraits at times feel unconsummated, to use a word that's all too apt in this context, and this can be frustrating, the literary equivalent of a series of first dates. But her approach also gets at the truth of how we experience, perceive, and remember romantic encounters, which are paradoxical at their core: superficial, and often fleeting, they also involve the deepest intimacies, and contain the possibility that they could evolve into a significant relationship or an incident tinged with menace. Maybe sex (or the promise of it) heightens our perceptions; maybe we're unusually vigilant as we attempt to judge this person, this moment, this potential relationship. Whatever the reason, our romantic liaisons frequently exist for us as a sharply observed collection of discrete details, like a director's establishing shot — a few salient particulars that sum up the object of our affection, his or her clothing, living space, and peculiar or memorable utterances or behavior. The fact that one man's bed "has a thin fitted sheet with broken elastic, so the sheet slips and slides all over the mattress," as Leonard writes. Or that he has an "odd way of kissing, without opening his mouth." The visit to the doctor's office, the lunch with an editor, are rarely etched with such precision.

Of course, once these incidents meet with the vagaries of memory and time, all that tends to remain of the people we've been with is a distilled assortment of details and sense memories rattling around in our minds. "He had a sleigh bed and a pennant from Dartmouth," Leonard writes. Or: "We go to the laundromat where he has a snow cone and reads Isherwood." Or: "His ceiling is draped in silk. His walls are hung with Tibetan flags." Paul, an actor and waiter, tells Elise, "I want to joust with you, so you always remember," as he hands her a lance. It's a humorous moment, but one of uncanny, idiot-savant-like emotional awareness: how true that in all likelihood this joust with him is the only thing she *will* remember of their date. (You can just hear a friend asking her, "Remember that guy who asked you to *joust*?") Memory also has a way of reducing people to their essence, like a piece of sea glass honed to a bright, beautiful nub. This is, needless to say, a process that's useful to a writer. "It seems to me," says Carter, an introspective, sensitive 16-year-old who later commits suicide, "that sometimes people, especially girls [...] have one beautiful little gesture they make, one characteristic thing." For Leonard, the statement is something like a literary ethos.

"I'm capturing the core of these relationships, or sometimes just the edge — when they blossom or fail," Leonard has said in an interview, and she has a knack for isolating the moment when a relationship's prevailing weather pattern shifts. These turning points also tend to stand out in our memories. Someone says a brutal, unforgivable thing. Someone's scary hidden self erupts. Alain, the gift-giver from Queens, yanks Elise by her hair and tosses her down his front stoop on New Year's Day. (She'd suspected her presence was upsetting his young daughters, and asked whether she should leave.) Andreas, a married Greek donut magnate, who has four children, an Orthodox wife, a private plane, and a yacht, goes with her to the Village Vanguard, and, when the lights go down, pinches her nipple, hard, crushing it. Timothy sneers at the idea of a baby, and when she goes to pick up her belongings, he has made a list of her pros and cons. *Pro: Great sex. Good person. Con:*

Needy, both emotionally and financially.

Leonard forgoes a chronological telling in favor of skipping around, following a private, internal logic. As I read, I couldn't decide whether the book suffered for this gnomic approach, or whether, as Leslie Jamison wrote in a *New Yorker* review of Chris Kraus's *I Love Dick*, another vaguely autobiographical novel about a woman's psychosexual life, "to organize events sequentially is to take away their power." Maybe, I thought, Leonard arranged the episodes according to the position of importance they occupy in her mind, or the repercussions they'd had on her life. A telling response on my part, since I could never shake the notion that *52 Men* was a memoir about Louise Wareham Leonard instead of a fictional work about Elise McKnight, so palpable is the tissue connecting it to reality. The celebrities and quasi-celebrities who appear, for instance — Michael, Jay, Lou, and Jonathan, as in Stipe, Carney, Reed, and Franzen — as well as those who have died (including the aforementioned Carter Cooper, Gloria Vanderbilt's son and Anderson's brother) are referred to by their actual first names, and further identified with revealing details. Jonathan is "the world's most famous North American novelist." "Lou," she sees in a hot tub and pretends not to recognize, despite the fact that, as she puts it, "'Sad Song' fashioned all my dreams."

Although some critics have faulted Leonard for her inconsistent stance on the truth — *Kirkus* said the book "straddles the line in a way that is irritating and perplexing," and an interviewer noted that the celebrities were "outed" on the cover — the demand for a foolish consistency betrays an ignorance about the ways in which fiction writers are always mining and transfiguring their lives (they just don't necessarily tip us off that they're doing it) and speaks to a basic, human, if sometimes prurient, desire: to know what actually happened. In interviews, Leonard has been transparent about the fact that she's writing from experience ("Every story is a man and a memory that lives with me all the time"), and my guess is the names, while providing a thrilling little frisson, are also nonfictional stakes tethering the stories to the real world. Did everything in them happen? Who knows? Who cares? Whatever license Leonard takes, these stories still bear the fingerprints of the author's lived experience; they deliver the visceral punch of reality.

They *feel* truthful, in part because, for all their weird specificity, they're almost eerily universal, a reminder of how pathetically unoriginal we human beings are when it comes to sex and love. I've had a man buy me a watch, and another promise to buy me a fancier one once we'd been together for a while. I've had several men tell me, as they tell Elise, "You're too angry," or "We are two very different people." And I have set off to travel with one only to realize I can't stand him. Indeed, one of the pleasures of reading this book is the snake charmer's way Leonard has of summoning your own experiences and memories. When Elise talks about Hewson, the finance guy who took her on six or seven dates but never kissed her, I am reminded of the writer who took me on six dates and then sent me an email insinuating that I should have made the first move. His note began, "I have little gray matter for matters of the heart." When she talks about E., who tells her he won't ever leave his marriage, I think of the married movie director who told me he was separated but went into the hotel room bathroom and called his wife, whispering to her in low, muffled, but distinguishable tones.

We all have such stories, and many of us have a deep and insistent urge to tell them. "We tell ourselves stories in order to live," Joan Didion wrote, in one of her most frequently quoted (and misunderstood) lines. She was talking about the stories we tell ourselves, the self-deception we practice as we impose meaning on the world around us. Leonard's book is about the stories we tell other people. We tell these stories precisely *because* everybody has them: they make people laugh, and they uncover wounds over which we bond. We tell them to get revenge on those who hurt us, and to redeem experiences that pained us. We tell them to brag: *somebody wanted us*. And we tell them because they're nostalgic reminders of lovers who were once close to us. But we also tell them for the pure narrative pleasure of it: relationship stories have a natural arc — beginning, middle, denouement, end — and characters we can sketch with a few deft marks. Romance makes writers of us all.

2.

IMPLICIT IN THIS NEED TO TELL is the idea that our stories say something fundamental about us, the tellers: that those we have loved, spent time with, mooned over, or slept with have helped to form who we are. These people have passed in and out of our lives, our psyches, our bodies. They have altered us with their words — criticism, praise, the sort of casual cruelties or keen but cutting observations only a lover would feel compelled to share. *52 Men* suggests that our identity is at least in part a product of our romantic past, and that the particulars we choose to depict that past are significant, comprising a kind of personal psychobiography.

The micro-tales in *52 Men* are all told in the first-person present tense, which means we don't get much in the way of authorial reflection. Leonard's focus is zoom-lens tight: she describes the various men, zeroing in on what they said and did — and how she responded — in a pivotal moment. Her alter ego, Elise McKnight, thus remains vaporous, enigmatic, elusive. At least one reviewer, a writer named Brian McGackin, who, probably not incidentally, has published a book called *Broetry* ("Ode to That Girl I Dated for, Like, a Month Sophomore Year"), has criticized McKnight for being a cipher: "goddess and muse and troubled shell of a nothing character defined only by the men who love her."

But maybe she's rather a woman who has had defining experiences with a range of men and chose to write about this slice of her life. The narrow scope is surely intentional, a literary and philosophical choice, the ultimate point of this controlled literary endeavor. The 52 men, in aggregate, convey a fair amount about the woman, Leonard-as-McKnight, whose life they have passed through, however glancingly. She appears to be an open, experimental person who seeks out a variety of paramours, not always wisely (a junkie saxophonist, an acrimonious rock star, a pugnacious Italian, an endearingly earnest businessman, a severely depressed artist, a bartender who has gone back to school, a graphic designer with a swing in his apartment), perhaps because they offer a dip into a variety of lives and attendant selves. She's chameleonlike, camouflaging herself to please this or that man. "As usual," she says, "I decide to win him over." She suffered a grievous early trauma, the aforementioned 53rd encounter — her stepbrother, Ben, started molesting her at age nine; in her late teens, their relationship turned sexual — and she's wounded, her actions arguably emanating from that anguish. Yet she's also slyly, coolly observant and has transformed her experiences into art, which is pretty much the opposite of being solely "defined by the men who love her." We know her, ultimately, through the book she has written. The narrative specifics she selects to describe the men are hers, as is the deadpan humor; all of it arises from *her* artistic consciousness. Although in style and tone *52 Men* differs from either Elizabeth Hardwick's *Sleepless Nights* or Renata Adler's *Speedboat*, it is, like both of these books, a novel of impressions unified by the author's sensibility.

If *52 Men* is a somewhat airless portrait of how one woman was shaped by — and has subsequently chosen to shape in narrative — the cavalcade of men in her life, Debra Monroe's memoir *My Unsentimental Education* (a cheeky nod to Flaubert) opens outward to provide a sociological or anthropological take on the same. Monroe, a professor at Texas State University and the author of six books, shows herself and her lovers to be actors played upon by historical, cultural, and societal forces. The book's central thesis, as it were, is the notion that romantic predilections are a product of the milieu one comes from, and that these don't necessarily change as one scales the ladder of social-class. Monroe, who was raised in Spooner, Wisconsin, a blue-collar town of bars and strip joints surrounded by farmland, writes about her higher education, both erotic and academic. For a woman among the first wave of female PhDs in early 1980s, especially one from a working-class background, the two were complicatedly intertwined. "Men I'd gone to school with had heard women were their equals. I'd heard this too. But it was recent news then," she writes in the prologue. "We'd all been raised in homes where women weren't. I usually dated down anyway, because dating up was work. [...] I chose men as if I'd never left home."

Home is where the first chapter begins. Monroe revisits her childhood in Spooner in the late '60s and early '70s, where she absorbed lessons about womanhood and its limited menu of possibilities. Although women's lib, as it was called then, was ascendant in other places, in rural Wisconsin women were expected to be a wife and mother ("I'd been raised, cultivated like a crop, to settle on a man," says Monroe), and maybe to work a little on the side. Monroe recalls her maternal grandmother giving her a scrapbook for Christmas; it contained a checklist titled "What I Want to Be When I Grow Up," with separate categories for boys and girls. "Mother," Monroe writes, "[was listed] as the first Girls' option, followed by Nurse, Teacher, Secretary, Stewardess. The Boys' options didn't list Father at all." And yet Monroe, who from an early age displayed an appetite for reading and a facility with words, sets off for college, to earn what will be her first of three degrees. Her mother gives her a typewriter as a graduation present, telling her, Monroe writes, "to remember I was training for a job that would last only until I had children, though later I might work part-time," at a "job that would move as my husband's job would move."

As far as husbands go, the examples she'd known left much to be desired. Her grandfather and father carouse, disappear for days, cheat. "That's marriage," her mother sighs. "It's never our turn." Her female relatives and the other women who briefly appear in the memoir (landlady, stepmother, mother-in-law) suffer the indignities heaped upon them because their husband is their identity, their power and influence in the world. Her grandmother, she says, "married a man who wasn't her equal in terms of ambition because ambition had added up to zilch without a man." When her father takes off for good, her mother tells her she would rather be widowed than divorced. Later, she marries a redneck monster who burdens her with debt, drinks to excess, routinely turns violent, and calls Monroe a cunt the first time he meets her. "Did I understand that being a middle-aged divorcée in a small, frozen town had made her feel redundant, a reverse spinster, without even a widow's status, so she'd taken the first man on offer?" Monroe writes, rhetorically quoting her mother. Suffice it to say, if there wasn't a societally sanctioned position for a single woman in lower-middle-class Midwestern America, there wasn't even an unsanctioned place for a woman with an academic career. While she's getting her master's degree, her father, an auto parts salesman, tells her, "You're educating yourself out of the marriage market."

PAT O'NEILL
UNTITLED (RHINOCEROS), 1985
GELATIN SILVER-PRINT, FRAMED
2.75 X 4"
UNIQUE
COURTESY CHERRY AND MARTIN, LOS ANGELES
PHOTO: BRIAN FORREST

Monroe didn't realize she was actually educating herself out of her social class, severing "the last conversational threads connecting me to my family." In her jaunty, wry, aphoristic, and aptly unsentimental style (which can occasionally veer toward wacky or clotted), she describes her quick and vertiginous jump between echelons. Her prose is brisk, propulsive, infectious, and formally befitting of her subject matter, as each chapter effectively covers a man and a new geographic locale. There's a boyfriend, 35 years old to her 18, who wears an eye patch and is wanted in Indiana for not paying child support. There's a husband, a country music musician with a secret illegitimate child, who leaves her the day of a Halloween party they are throwing together. There's another husband, a shiftless, untruthful, spendthrift sociopath with the irascible temper of a teenager, whose first instinct is always to throw a punch. "School had been a time of growing into one life and then another, another, changing social backdrops, lovers, husbands, each time hoping my new life would be the last revision," she writes, verbalizing the whiplash-inducing speed with which the scenery of her existence changes during those years.

The stressful push-pull of performing her new, educated self — upon receiving her PhD, she gets a professorship at the University of North Carolina — and slipping back into the comforts of her old, provincial self forms the central tension of this book. What happens when the way you were raised is fundamentally at odds with the mores of where you are headed? Even while she is reading, writing, grading student papers, studying for exams, acing job interviews, and winning the Flannery O'Connor Award for her short stories, Monroe is sleeping with, dating, and marrying layabouts, hustlers, and small-time drug dealers. A professor, she tells us, once described her as "reasonably intelligent, but with unaccountably bad taste in men." But her bad taste, such as it is, is in fact quite plainly accounted for in the memoir. It arises from growing up in a place where retrograde gender roles were the norm, from an inability to harmonize her intellectual and libidinous selves, from her superego tussling with her id. She longs for someone who can discuss her work or contemplate Lucretius with her, but with whom she also has "luxuriant, frantic, slaking" sex. "I wanted a man who'd match my old self, my new self, all my selves," she writes. "So far I'd met Either and Or."

My Unsentimental Education is at root a meditation on identity, on the irresolvable and often heartbreaking chasm that opens up inside oneself when one is caught between two different social classes. "The distance between my aspiring daytime self and my nighttime self had widened," Monroe writes. I too was raised in the lower-middle-class Midwest. The towns I grew up in, in Iowa and

Illinois, were neither blue-collar nor rural, but they were predominantly working-class, and far from the wealthy, intellectual milieus that were home to my classmates at the Ivy League college I attended. Once there, I found myself unable to convey the social challenges and humiliations of college to my family: I didn't know what a phallic symbol was, had never read *The New Yorker* or ordered Japanese food or eaten fresh, not canned, pears. But I also found it impossible to talk to my classmates about where I'd come from. Few of them had backgrounds similar to my own. A persistent, nagging sense of alienation plagued me; my cultural referents and financial constraints were so exotic to my peers. I felt inadequate, embarrassed about all I didn't know or hadn't experienced, unable to relate. (Monroe: "When he realized I had never traveled, just moved, that I didn't know opera, he stopped.")

Dating — "hooking up," as we called it — distilled the whole dilemma. The men I met had lifestyles I idealized, country houses and boarding schools and parents who were therapists or professors or businesspeople who held dinner parties and attended charity events. And yet these men also seemed ridiculously sheltered and effete to me, and I never felt I could be truthful with them about the disorientation I was experiencing. In one passage, writing about her schizophrenic grandmother, Monroe notes that schizophrenia is statistically high among first- and second-generation immigrants, and says, "researchers speculate that, for those predisposed, the radical stress of dividing the self between one world and its rules and another world and its rules serves as trigger." This is a metaphor, obviously, for Monroe's own psychic disassociation. If she beats this drum a bit hard at times ("I split myself in two," she says, late in the book, and I scrawled in the margins, *WE GET IT*), it's understandable, as this was the central quandary of her adulthood.

Upon first reading these books, I could anticipate a kind of knee-jerk feminist critique of the authors' focus on male lovers, boyfriends, and husbands as a lens through which to view their lives. (Although readers of any persuasion might relate to either book, Leonard and Monroe are heterosexual women expressly talking about men.) *What a limited way of viewing women, when they are so much more than the men they are with*, this view goes. *Why not focus on their professional and artistic accomplishments?* True, women are no longer defined by marriage in the way they were for centuries, in the way that Monroe's mother felt she was as recently as the 1980s. And these books are not chick lit: the quest for an engagement that culminates in marriage is not the organizing principle of either character's existence. Still, both books also make the point that women are nevertheless profoundly affected by the men they choose. We may no longer be defined by whom we marry, but when people are spending nearly a decade or more of adult life unattached, our romantic experiences necessarily play a critical role in the formation of the self. "We are, all of us, molded and remolded by those who have loved us," Françoise Mauriac wrote in *The Desert of Love*, a book I read years ago when I was studying French literature in college, "and though that love may pass, we remain none the less *their* work — a work that very likely they do not recognize, and which is never exactly what they intended."

In their own way, both of these writers show how lovers can leave lasting scars. This or that man in *52 Men* is always diagnosing Elise McKnight, telling her what her issues are, emphasizing that they can't help her — *it's not their fault.* "You are troubled and obviously on medication and at first I hardly recognized you," says Jay, the magazine intern who "will be press secretary to a President." When she starts to cry during sex, Charlie the saxophonist says, "I can't touch you … You're hurt, too hurt," and turns away from her in bed. "You remind me of everything I hate about women," Michael the rock star pronounces, when she takes him up on his invitation to visit. Reading all this, you think back to the ridiculous or disparaging things men have said to you ("Why can't you be sweet?") and the regrettable, though maybe deserved, things you have said in return. Because Elise isn't merely a passive receptacle: "*I cannot take your pain*," she writes to one man, and several others she simply leaves. When she breaks up with Klaus, a German guy from school, he cuts the eyes out of a photo of her and sends it to her in the mail. It's an image that evokes the psychic wounds we all inflict on the people we're intimate with. Neither party comes away unscathed.

Characteristically, Monroe doesn't dwell on the psychological repercussions of bad partners, but her memoir is an incredible catalog of the practical difficulties they caused her. Physically: One tries to choke her when she breaks up with him. Another pushes her down the stairs while they are taking LSD. Her second husband, Chet, swings at the slightest provocation. Geographically: Her first husband, whom she never names, moves to Kansas with her and then leaves her, not long after, to shoulder their shared lease and piles of bills alone. Chet, unemployed and unfulfilled, begs to leave North Carolina, where Monroe is a professor; she finds a new job in Texas, and he doesn't move with her. Financially: Chet has her apply for credit cards in her name and then spends profligately; she has to work a second job waitressing to pay down their debt. Almost lethally: Chet has her take out an expensive life insurance policy, then tampers with the brakes on her car so she nearly crashes. Monroe briskly acknowledges how easy it is to get irrevocably entangled with another person: "I'd hurtled through someone else's history," she says of her second husband. "Near miss. Almost mine." Yet she's also insistent that her bad-news significant others had some positive, if unintended, consequences. Had her relationships flourished, she would not have pursued work with such zeal. At one point, she tells a professor she's getting a PhD because "no one's around to mind."

My Unsentimental Education leaves readers convinced that Monroe's deadbeat lovers and romantic tribulations are knotted up with the creation of her successful, intellectual self in ways that can never be untangled. As she writes, quoting John Steinbeck's *Grapes of Wrath*: "How will we know it's us without our past?"

3.

In that pleasingly strange way the various projects you're working on start cross-pollinating among themselves, as I was reading for this piece, I also began writing a personal essay about the men I met up with while traveling alone in Europe the summer I graduated from college. I found myself struggling not only with what I considered to be an embarrassingly antiquated reticence when it came to writing about sex — *would a young woman's sexual escapades be distasteful to some readers?* — but also with the formal challenge of structuring the story. To me, it read like a string of unconnected episodes: *and then and then and then*. After several days spent stalled and weepy, I decided to go meta and wrote: *What unifies a narrative about a character pitching from one romantic adventure to another? How do you prevent it from reading like a desultory chain of episodic affairs, devoid of plot, theme, or intrinsic order? How to write about a libidinous, searching, mischievous character who also happens to be a woman?*

When men write about their sexual adventures, there's a name for it, a genre: the picaresque narrative. "I myself am in a very old tradition, namely, that of the picaresque novel," William Burroughs said in a 1974 interview, with all the bravado one would expect. "People complain that my novels have no plot. Well a picaresque novel has no plot. It is simply a series of incidents." The most succinct definition of the picaresque I've found is that of the late Orville Prescott, erstwhile book critic for *The New York Times*; a picaresque, he wrote in his 1953 review of Saul Bellow's *The Adventures of Augie March*, is a first-person account of "the adventures of a rogue held together only by the personality of its hero, with no unifying structure or situation." In a picaresque tale, the protagonist tends to be fatherless, of modest origins, an outsider, a trickster, a social climber. He rambles around having adventures, sometime of the romantic sort. Think Augie March, Don Juan, Tom Jones, and the numerous other aimless, charmingly dissolute male heroes of Western literature.

By those dictates, *52 Men* and *My Unsentimental Education* are picaresque narratives. Both consist of a series of incidents not driven by an overarching plot. Neither is, in Monroe's words, "an old-fashioned story with coincidences and mirage-like continuity." And both characters, Monroe and Elise McKnight, are itinerant, deracinated, distant from their families, essentially alone in the world, and improvising as they go. "I'd lived all over, and I'd lived by my wits, making choices by myself," writes Monroe, who called five states home in as many years. About the men she got involved with, she says, "If I turned out to be wrong, having based my decision on who was locally available, on who suited my past if not my present or future, I alone was responsible, alone." Elise, who at one point describes herself as "completely free," roams mostly around New York, but she also travels to Mississippi, North Carolina, New Zealand, Montauk. It's not a stretch to call Monroe and Leonard-as-McKnight sexual explorers, seekers, though perhaps not by design. As Monroe puts it: "I hadn't meant to be a 'sexual adventuress' as I've heard Edna St. Vincent Millay and Martha Gellhorn described."

It seemed like a remarkable coincidence that I was sent these two books while I was thinking about the idea of the female picaresque as I tried to shape my own essay — there isn't exactly a robust tradition of picaresque narratives by or about women. There's Daniel Defoe's *Moll Flanders*, arguably, though it's obviously written by a man. Virginia Woolf's *Orlando*, though the heroine is first a hero, and her adventures are of an aristocratic stripe. Erica Jong's *Fear of Flying*, whose protagonist, Isadora Wing, leaves her husband and romps around Europe. Her successors these days are probably found in the realm of memoir: Elizabeth Gilbert's *Eat, Pray, Love* and Cheryl Strayed's *Wild*. There are a scattered few more — Amy Bloom's novels, *Lucky Us* and *Away*; Angela Carter's *Nights at the Circus* — but the point is that the picaresque has traditionally been an unrelievedly masculine genre. Of the 101 books mentioned on Goodreads's list of "Best all time picaresque novels," at the time of this writing, 95 are by men.

That's not really surprising, since only in the past few decades have most women been able to move alone through the world. To light out for the territory, to hit the road, one needs freedom and mobility above all, and yet for much of history, women have been bound by familial and societal obligations, and from a very young age. They were also more vulnerable to physical danger, and castigated more harshly for flouting society's orthodoxies and rules. Only with the greater personal and sexual liberation of the late 1960s and 1970s would a woman drifting from exploit to exploit have been a realistic fictional conceit.

Even today, when most women are fundamentally independent and living as they choose, many of us still don't feel free to write openly about our sex lives, or to announce our refusal to conform to societal norms. You have only to go on the internet to see that slut-shaming is a real phenomenon and that women who dare to thumb their nose at convention are often very harshly judged. As Kathryn Schulz wrote in her excellent profile of Cheryl Strayed in *New York* magazine, "In a culture with profoundly ambivalent feelings about independent women, it is not always clear what kind of adventures we will be lauded for undertaking, nor what kind of tales we will be lauded for telling."

I thought of this when I read Mr. Broetry call the first half of *52 Men* "a Gwyneth Paltrow sexual humble brag." The characterization irked me because of the double standard it contains. When a man talks about the women he's slept with, he's just talking about his conquests, his sexual exploits — men are not only allowed to brag, braggadocio is expected from them. But how is a woman supposed to write about her past if it's unseemly or boastful to say she's been the object of desire? In a related aside about the "inconsistencies" of the sexual revolution and the hypocritical criteria by which women are judged, Monroe writes that women "weren't supposed to pile up a 'number,' the new term for copious notches on the bedpost that men are improved by having."

However, when women do risk entering the fray to tell their stories, they tend to be received with enthusiasm. There is clearly a ravenous hunger for more books and shows and films that reflect the truth of women's lives. This is why *Sex and the City* garnered such a large and obsessive fan base during its six-year run; its characters talked candidly, even vulgarly, about sex, portraying it as just another vital element of a woman's existence. It's why *Eat, Pray, Love* and *Wild* became massive bestsellers and were made into hit movies: Gilbert and Strayed dared to be frank about their appetites, their discontents, and their rejection of tradition. The dearth of such portrayals, still, is why Monroe's and Leonard's books still feel a tad revolutionary, even in 2016. And it's also why when women write about their erotic adventures the tales have a different resonance and cultural impact than those written by men.

Of course, in any discussion of women's stories, it's crucial to note that they also carry their distinctive emotional and cultural weight because they are so often tales of assault, violence, and abuse. But while abuse is obviously present in both books, I'm reluctant to classify either as a narrative of trauma sustained and overcome. Both women have indeed triumphed, in some sense, but through art, which is mysterious and unpredictable and cannot be easily reduced to causes and effects, perpetrators and victims. Monroe, who lived through a country music album's worth of bad men and harrowing ordeals, rejects the premise outright: "By today's standards, using one-size-fits-all diagnostics, he was abusive. But I never thought his anger was my fault. I never felt helpless, or not for long." (In October, she penned an essay for *Kirkus* bemoaning the vogue for equating memoir with therapeutic tales of recovery and the resultant narrowing of the genre.) Her quirky, fast-paced book doesn't read like a recovery memoir at all, so averse is she to psychologizing and so crisply and efficiently does she dispatch with emotion, like the native Midwesterner she is.

Leonard recounts a handful of truly disturbing incidents: she wakes up to one man having sex with her, even after she told him no; about another, she writes, "It isn't rape exactly. It isn't consensual either." Some of these encounters seem to replicate her early trauma; others appear to offer a kind of balm or escape ("the water is green and salty and rushes in solid sweeping walls against us"). In an interview, Leonard has said that she views the second part of the book, about Elise's stepbrother's abuse — fictional, she emphasizes — as an "explosion" and "the 52 men the result or 'fallout' of that explosion." But it's interesting she chose to structure the book so that we read about the childhood trauma *after* we read about the 52 men — our judgment is not colored, and we don't come to easy conclusions. The book, to Leonard's great credit, rarely draws stark lines. Elise is sometimes the wounded, sometimes the one who wounds. Like most of us who wade into the emotional deep and come back with stories to tell, she is probably both.

THE WRITING OF LIFE

MARTIN WOESSNER

IT WAS A LITTLE OVER A YEAR AGO that I made my first visit to the Harry Ransom Center at the University of Texas at Austin. Taking advantage of the winter break from teaching, and desperately needing an excuse to get out of town, I descended upon one of the finest collections of literary manuscripts in the country, if not the world. I didn't realize it then, but I was both fleeing my life and trying to save it at the same time, doing the one thing I've ever done well: reading. I was seeking out the traces of a writer in whose words I had found solace once before. Secretly, subconsciously, I must have been hoping that a dose of literary therapy would work its magic on me once again.

"So you're here to work on the David Foster Wallace Papers?" the cheerful receptionist asked. Admittedly, I wore the well-worn boots and shapeless sweater, not to mention the glasses and the beard, of a grad student who has spent more time with *Infinite Jest* than with actual human beings in the world. I couldn't help but smirk at the assumption.

"No," I replied. "I'm here to look at the Coetzee collection." I could see her recalibrating her initial assessment of me. "Oh," she said. "There are a few others here working on him as well." And with that, I was ushered into the inner sanctum of the reading room.

There were at least five of us exploring the vast archive of Coetzee's papers now held by the Ransom Center, making up roughly half of the reading room's residents that week. A couple others were communing with the spirit of Foster Wallace, while one fellow consulted old detective novels and still another lady examined what appeared to be architectural or landscape designs of some kind. Some of these researchers had traveled great distances to Austin — from the United Kingdom, from Australia. I thought I heard somebody say that they drove up from Houston, surely the most treacherous journey of all. (I made that trip only once myself, to see Elliott Smith way back when.)

Fifty years earlier, J. M. Coetzee had journeyed to Austin from faraway South Africa, by way of England, where he was working temporarily as a computer programmer after having written an MA thesis on Ford Madox Ford, which he submitted to the University of Cape Town in 1963.

Coetzee arrived at the University of Texas in the fall of 1965 to pursue a PhD in linguistics and literature. What would eventually become the Ransom Center was less than a decade old then, but it was already gobbling up manuscripts and artifacts of immense cultural value at an astounding pace. The works of James Joyce and Samuel Beckett were early prizes, and at one point Martin Heidegger's original draft of *Sein und Zeit* was about to join them, in a deal almost brokered by Hannah Arendt. At the Ransom Center today you can peruse collections stretching from Jorge Luis Borges to Gloria Swanson, or from Doris Lessing to Don DeLillo. There's older stuff, too: Chaucer, Shakespeare, a Gutenberg Bible. Coetzee's archive, needless to say, is in very good company.

As I familiarized myself with Coetzee's clear and careful penmanship, poring over draft after handwritten draft, I couldn't help but imagine him doing something similar decades earlier, as he deciphered Beckett's scrawl. His dissertation was on Beckett, and he utilized the collection of his manuscripts obtained by the Ransom Center. But, having read J. C. Kannemeyer's exhaustive biography *J. M. Coetzee: A Life in Writing*, I knew that the author I was chasing did more in Austin than sit around and read Beckett. I knew, for instance, that he was also collecting materials — both in the library and well beyond it — that would eventually find their way into his first work of fiction, *Dusklands*, which appeared in 1974, some three years after Coetzee's involuntary return to South Africa.

Perhaps because its primary themes are still so relevant today, *Dusklands* remains a dazzling work of fiction. It explores legacies of imperialism, madness, racism, and military brutality via two separate but necessarily entwined stories. Coetzee started drafting the second story, "The Narrative of Jacobus Coetzee," first, in Buffalo, where he had landed his first academic appointment at the State University of New York. It passes itself off as a historical palimpsest. It contains the violent and racist first-person account of an early 18th-century Dutch colonist in the Cape, one Jacobus Coetzee, which has been "edited" by an S. J. Coetzee, who also provides a brief afterword. The "translator" of these texts, who also appends a brief preface to the work, is listed as J. M. Coetzee. But nothing is what it seems. Jacobus Coetzee was in fact a real historical personage, whose travel accounts J. M. Coetzee had read while studying in Austin (and to whom he was in fact distantly related), but the central "Narrative" in *Dusklands* is a work of fiction, not historical fact. The same goes for the editor's afterword and the translator's preface. The same goes, in fact, for the editor and the translator themselves. The J. M. Coetzee who was the "translator" of "The Narrative of Jacobus Coetzee" both was and was not the J. M. Coetzee whose name could be found on the cover of *Dusklands*.

Just who, exactly, was this J. M. Coetzee, and from where did he come? Was he owning up to his Afrikaner heritage in *Dusklands* or distancing himself from it? What some might see as postmodern play, as a kind of formalist gamesmanship underscoring the so-called "death of the author" — something akin to Borges's classic short story "Borges and I" or even the lesser incarnations of it today in the seemingly confessional writings of a Ben Lerner or a Sheila Heti — was in fact just the opposite. It was what Coetzee scholar David Attwell, in his marvelous new book *J. M. Coetzee and the Life of Writing: Face-to-Face with Time*, calls "a huge existential enterprise, grounded in fictionalized autobiography."

In an oft-cited remark — from an earlier interview with Attwell, actually — Coetzee once declared that "all autobiography is storytelling, all writing is autobiography," which seems to complicate, not dismiss, the whole idea of authorship, including the very ideas of authorial intent and responsibility. When Eugene Dawn, a technocratic cog in the vast American military-industrial complex who narrates the other story in *Dusklands*, "The Vietnam Project," expresses "high hopes of finding out whose fault I am," we might be forgiven for thinking that he, Dawn, who cracks under the pressure of writing a dissertation-like report on wartime propaganda tactics, has more than a little bit of J. M. Coetzee in him — or at least as much as his "manager," an "ordinary man" he loathes by the name of Coetzee.

Navigating one's way through this authorial hall of mirrors is difficult. Even with the cardinal points of biography, autobiography, writing, and storytelling in view, it is easy to get lost in the unchartered territory between the life and the fictionalization of that life in the literary work. I suppose it is reassuring to know that, most of the time, Coetzee himself didn't necessarily know where the one began and the other ended. Among the priceless treasures in the neatly organized boxes of his papers at the Ransom Center are little notebooks in which he recorded, rather regularly, his reflections on the creative process: a stray observation here, a fully formed self-critique there, as if he were subjecting his own writing to an internalized academic analysis. Often, he had no idea where a story was taking him until he actually got there, and the notebooks record his frustrations with false starts and imaginative dead ends along the way. But surely Coetzee's routine of daily writing took him through familiar territory. Now that we have access to some of his papers, and now that biographical accounts are starting to give us a glimpse of his existence beyond the page, we can see how Coetzee's life provided the seeds — if not the fully formed forest — for almost all of his fictional output.

There are at least two ways to survey this terrain, and, conveniently enough, Kannemeyer's and Attwell's books represent them. The subtle difference in their titles reflects what is in fact a rather wide divergence in their respective approaches. Kannemeyer's massive tome promises "a life in writing," whereas Attwell's more nimble study investigates "the life of writing." The former focuses on the biography and autobiography, and uses the writing and storytelling to illuminate them, whereas the latter looks first at the writing and the storytelling, and utilizes the biography and the autobiography to unlock their secrets. Kannemeyer, in other words, uses the fiction to get at the life, but Attwell uses the life to get at the fiction. If one boils the fiction down to its biographical components, then the other tracks the transformation of the flesh-and-blood life into the fictional worlds of the novels. Both approaches produce fascinating results, but Attwell's captures more of the magic that is the creative process — a magic that still seemed to cling to the various notebooks, drafts, and clippings I felt and held, gingerly and maybe too reverently, in Austin.

For many years, Coetzee wrote out his drafts, longhand, in exam booklets from the University of Cape Town, where he taught English literature. It was at Cape Town where Attwell, who is currently a professor of English at the University of York, in England, earned his MA in African literary theory and criticism. Coetzee was his supervisor. Like his supervisor, Attwell went on to Austin to earn his PhD at the University of Texas. It's safe to say that few other scholars know as much about Coetzee the man and the author as he does. His previous works — such as Coetzee's *Doubling the Point* (1992), a collection of essays and interviews Attwell edited and conducted, and his own *J. M. Coetzee: South Africa and the Politics of Writing* (1993) — have become indispensible points of reference in Coetzee studies. Given all this, and given that he was the first scholar to be granted access to the papers now deposited at the Ransom, even before they were available to the general public thanks to Coetzee's own intervention, Attwell was well positioned to write yet another important book. But what he has produced in *J. M. Coetzee and the Life of Writing* is something that transcends the usual academic monograph. At times, it reads more like a primer on how literary works come into being than anything else, a profound meditation on what it means to take up writing as a way of life rather than yet another scholarly study of this or that discourse in this or that novel.

Much of Coetzee's work has been described as cold or clinical — academic even. His prose is sparse; his aesthetic vision steely, even harsh. Coetzee's novels depict bleak environs and are populated with characters who seem to be only one or two steps removed from Jacobus Coetzee and Eugene Dawn: deluded or delusional colonists, boring bureaucrats, lonely professors, cranky old authors — hardly the kind of people who might engender warm and fuzzy attachment on the part of readers. Just think of Magda, the narrator of *In the Heart of the Country* (1977); or the magistrate in *Waiting for the Barbarians* (1980) if not also the protagonist of *Life & Times of Michael K* (1983); or Elizabeth Curren or David Lurie in *Age of Iron* (1990) and *Disgrace* (1999), respectively.

And of course there is Elizabeth Costello, the character who became Coetzee's performative alter ego in the late '90s and beyond, when, in lieu of delivering public lectures in his own voice, Coetzee would often read stories about Costello, an aging and sometimes cantankerous Australian academic and writer who seemed to have much, though not everything, in common with Coetzee, including his vegetarianism and his concern for the welfare of animals. Coetzee's Tanner Lectures at Princeton, which were published as *The Lives of Animals* in 1999, offered us a character who was at once noble and frail, persuasive and disagreeable, determined and yet full of self-doubt. She may be the most realistic character Coetzee has ever created, yet she often rails against "realism," as was the case with "What Is Realism?," the first story in which she appeared, a piece read by Coetzee as the Ben Belitt Lecture at Bennington College in Vermont in 1996.

At almost every turn, Attwell emphasizes the profoundly personal and affective origins of Coetzee's novels. This may come as a surprise to scholars who think that everything Coetzee has written is simply too academic — a fictionalization of postcolonial theory, for example, or a meandering sociopolitical parable of some kind. The novels may indeed be these things, but they are also traces of an extremely self-conscious, engaged, and self-aware life. *In the Heart of the Country*, for example, is a pastoral novel about the genre of pastoral novels, but it is also, Attwell argues, a kind of self-administered therapy, the first of Coetzee's many "swansongs to the Karoo," his ancestral homeland in South Africa. It undermines the very genre out of which it stems and externalizes Coetzee's conflicted attachment to the landscape that shaped some of his earliest and happiest memories, despite also being a landscape indelibly marked by generations of settler colonialism.

Similarly, *Age of Iron*, which tackles nothing less than the cruel and deforming heritage of apartheid and Afrikaner identity, is as much about Coetzee's own relationship with his mother, transformed into the character of Elizabeth Curren, as it is about social upheaval and political change. *The Master of Petersburg* (1994), in which Coetzee reimagines a historical Dostoevsky searching for clues of the last hours of his stepson, who had fallen to his death, is a postmodern reworking of *The Possessed*, laden with intertextual fireworks — but it is also a profound statement, in fictionalized form, of Coetzee's own grief over the death of his only son Nicolas, who had also fallen to his death from an apartment balcony in Johannesburg just two years before work on the manuscript began. "The novel is," as Attwell describes it, "a personal document seeking to become impersonal, and only partly succeeding" — a work of "autobiographical historical fiction, if that is imaginable." Like Dostoevsky before him, Coetzee was trying "to write his son into immortality," fully aware of the painful impossibility of just such an endeavor.

Far from diminishing the power of these novels, Attwell's careful reconstructions of their respective evolutions demonstrate just how meticulous and multifaceted Coetzee's artistic vision has been, from *Dusklands* all the way up to his most recent work, *The Childhood of Jesus* (2013). Even his most expressly political novels, such as *Disgrace* (1999), have grown out of deeply personal emotions and entanglements — in this case a father's relationship with his daughter, Gisela. Attwell's study, which will appeal not just to Coetzee scholars but to anybody interested in the writerly life, focuses primarily on what is now being referred to as Coetzee's South African period, roughly from around 1974 to about 2002, when he officially moved to Adelaide, Australia, but it touches upon just about every piece of fiction that Coetzee has written, including, naturally, the triumvirate of fictionalized autobiographies: *Boyhood* (1997), *Youth* (2002), and *Summertime* (2009). In showing how Coetzee has turned his life into art, Attwell demonstrates that the life of writing, arduous and isolating as it is, can nevertheless be a meaningful, purposeful, fundamentally ethical endeavor of the highest order. But only if the life of writing faces up to its most dangerous and difficult task: the writing of life.

Throughout his career, Coetzee has been a scrupulous self-examiner but an ambivalent fictionalizer. "I have no interest in telling stories," he confided in one of his working notebooks while toiling away on what would become *Waiting for the Barbarians*, "it is the process of storytelling that interests me." Hence his penchant for always attempting to introduce — as Attwell puts it — "greater self-consciousness" into his writing. Attwell sees Coetzee as consistently "bearing witness" to his own "existence in the act of writing" throughout his career as a novelist — a kind of ongoing confession by other means, if you will. Sometimes this has entailed a process of addition or alteration, an attempt to put some part of himself directly into the thing he was writing. Most often, though, it has taken the shape of surgically precise editorial excisions, which occluded the very personal and intellectual motivations that animated the composition of the work in the first place. Looking closely at the countless drafts that Coetzee produced for each and every one of his novels, Attwell rightly concludes that, for this Nobel Prize winner at least, "deletion" is in fact "central to the process of invention." If Foster Wallace is a patron saint of imaginative and expansive self-expression, Coetzee carries the banner for the relentless artistry of subtraction — a skill that, in these days of social media–induced oversharing, is surely slipping from view.

I went to Austin to find traces of America's impact on Coetzee's fiction. I spent much of my time on materials relating to "The Vietnam Project." I knew that Coetzee had opposed American involvement in Vietnam; that he had submitted a satire of Swiftian proportions to the UT student newspaper deriding American military strategy at the time; and that his visa wasn't renewed because he participated in faculty protests at Buffalo, which were held in support of student antiwar demonstrators. But I had no idea that much of his reading of American fiction, from William Faulkner to William S. Burroughs and Norman Mailer, was also filtered through the lens of the village massacres and napalm bombings taking place half the world away, televised, on occasion, for the nightly news. I had no idea that Coetzee had actually read, and carefully at that, the writings of Herman Kahn and other think-tank intellectuals who pushed the world toward policies of mutually assured destruction. There are traces of all these things in the published version of "The Vietnam Project," of course, but you need a pretty powerful magnifying glass to see them. Once you look at the drafts and notes now at the Ransom Center, though, these precedents all but jump off the page.

What I also didn't anticipate finding in Austin was evidence that stories such as "The Vietnam Project" reflected not just Coetzee's reading or his politics, but his most intimate personal life as well. The collapse of Eugene Dawn's marriage, a somewhat minor subplot in the final version of the story, was in fact the primary focus of Coetzee's initial sketches, which consisted almost entirely of dialogue between a therapist and an unfaithful, unhappy wife, who spends her session complaining about her husband, and about men in general. I didn't even have to speculate about the source material for these sketches, since traces of Coetzee's own quarrels with his wife were right there in his notes. By the time the story was finished, though, all of this had been either deleted or omitted. The slate had been wiped clean — or almost clean, anyway.

"The Vietnam Project," which began as an exorcism of marital strife, became on a much larger scale an exorcism of imperial madness. Sitting there in the reading room of the Ransom Center, I couldn't help thinking that, at root, both evils were symptoms of the same psychological or spiritual malady, that a poisonous personal life merely mirrored the brutal realities of the world in which we live. Microcosm, macrocosm, it's all one in the same. But was I contemplating Coetzee's life or my own?

Despite the obvious differences between our respective lives and times, I was nevertheless struck by the underlying, unchanging similarities. The Vietnam War may have come to a close, apartheid may have ended, but the hatreds animating both were still with us. Not much had changed, I thought, in the 45 years since Coetzee started writing, on the first of January, 1970, in a cold basement in Buffalo. Now, as then, racism remains a vicious social virus, plaguing the body politic. Now, as then, imperial violence flashes across the television screen. Now, as then, a cold and calculating rationalism seems to deform our most intimate relations with other people. Now, as then, there is too much cruelty in the world. I'd like to think that we can write ourselves out of all this, that writing and storytelling might save us somehow. But that would mean coming face-to-face not just with time, but also, and more terrifyingly, with ourselves. And honestly, how much of ourselves can we bear to reveal — or not reveal, as the case may be?

MICHAEL J. AGOVINO is the author of *The Bookmaker: A Memoir of Money, Luck, and Family from the Utopian Outskirts of New York City* and *The Soccer Diaries: An American's Thirty-Year Pursuit of the International Game.*

HISHAM BUSTANI was born in 1975 in Amman, Jordan, and has four published collections of short fiction. He has been described as "bringing a new wave of surrealism to [Arabic] literary culture, which missed the surrealist revolution of the last century." He has collaborated across artistic disciplines, working to bring literature together with music, painting, contemporary dance, and hip-hop. Bustani's work has been translated into five languages, and has appeared in *World Literature Today, The Common,* and *The Literary Review.* His book *The Perception of Meaning* was awarded the 2014 University of Arkansas Arabic Translation Award and was published by Syracuse University Press in 2015.

MARCI CALABRETTA CANCIO-BELLO is the author of *Hour of the Ox,* which won the 2015 AWP Donald Hall Prize for Poetry, and *Last Train to the Midnight Market* (2013), and has received poetry fellowships from Kundiman and the Knight Foundation, among others. Her work has appeared or is forthcoming in *Best New Poets 2015, Columbia: A Journal of Literature & Art, Narrative Magazine, Southern Humanities Review,* and more. She serves as co-founder and managing editor for *Print-Oriented Bastards,* a contributing editor for *The Florida Book Review,* and producer for *The Working Poet Radio Show.* Visit her at www.marcicalabretta.com.

MIKE DAVIS is a contributing editor at the *Los Angeles Review of Books* and the author of *Planet of Slums, City of Quartz, In Praise of Barbarians,* and more than a dozen other books. He teaches at the University of California, Riverside.

COLIN DAYAN is Robert Penn Warren Professor in the Humanities and Professor of Law at Vanderbilt University. Her recent books include *The Law Is a White Dog: How Legal Rituals Make and Unmake Persons, The Story of Cruel and Unusual,* and, most recently, *With Dogs at the Edge of Life.* She is a member of the American Academy of Arts and Sciences.

JAY DESHPANDE is the author of *Love the Stranger* (YesYes Books, 2015). He was selected by Billy Collins for the 2015 Scotti Merrill Memorial Award at the Key West Literary Seminar. Poems have appeared in *Boston Review, Sixth Finch, Handsome, Prelude, The Offing,* and elsewhere. He works as a freelance writer for publications including *Slate* and *The New Republic,* and lives in Brooklyn.

NATALIE EILBERT is the author of the debut poetry collection *Swan Feast* (Bloof Books, 2015). She is also the author of two chapbooks, *Conversation with the Stone Wife* (Bloof Books, 2014) and *And I Shall Again Be Virtuous* (Big Lucks Books, 2014). Her work has appeared in or is forthcoming from *The New Yorker, Tin House, Poem-a-Day, The Kenyon Review,* and elsewhere. She is the founding editor of *The Atlas Review.*

ANIKA FAJARDO was born in Colombia and raised in Minnesota. Her writing has appeared in various publications and earned awards from the Minnesota State Arts Board, the Loft Literary Center, and the Jerome Foundation.

AMANDA FORTINI has written for *The New York Times, The New Yorker, Rolling Stone, New York* magazine, *Slate,* and *Salon,* among other publications, and she is a contributing editor at *Elle Magazine.* Her essays have been widely anthologized, including in *Best American Political Writing.* She lives in Livingston, Montana.

BENJAMIN HALE is the author of the novel *The Evolution of Bruno Littlemore* (Twelve, 2011) and the forthcoming collection *The Fat Artist* (Simon & Schuster, 2016). He has received the Bard Fiction Prize, a Michener-Copernicus Award, and nominations for the Dylan Thomas Prize and the New York Public Library's Young Lions Fiction Award. His fiction and nonfiction have appeared, among other places, in *Conjunctions, Harper's Magazine, The New York Times, The Washington Post, Dissent, The L Magazine, The Millions,* and has been anthologized in *The Best American Science and Nature Writing 2013.* He is a senior editor of *Conjunctions* and currently teaches at Bard College.

ANNE JOLIS, previously a reporter and editor for *The Wall Street Journal,* is a writer and animation student based in New York.

SARAH LINDSAY is a Lannan Literary Fellow and author of four books of poetry, most recently *Debt to the Bone-Eating Snotflower* from Copper Canyon Press. Her work has received a Pushcart Prize and the Carolyn Kizer Prize, and has appeared in *Poetry, The New York Times, Parnassus,* and others. She is employed as a copyeditor in Greensboro.

HELEN MALMGREN is a freelance writer and reporter. Her investigative stories have won numerous awards, including two Emmys and a George Foster Peabody Award.

GOENAWAN MOHAMAD is founder and editor of *Tempo* magazine, Indonesia's most respected news magazine. It was banned by the Suharto government in 1994 after publishing details of the government's purchase of aging East German destroyers, a confidential subject of dispute among Suharto's cabinet members. In 1995, Mohamad founded the Institute for the Studies on Free Flow of Information (ISAI), which produced alternative media intended to circumvent censorship. Mohamad later formed the Alliance of Independent Journalists, the only independent journalism organization in Indonesia. Following Suharto's resignation in May 1998, Mohamad led a group of reporters in restarting *Tempo* online and in print. Mohamad was a 1990 Nieman fellow at Harvard University and in 1997 received the Nieman fellows' Louis Lyons Award for Conscience and Integrity in Journalism. In 1998, he was awarded the Committee to Protect Journalists' International Press Freedom Award. Mohamad is a visiting history professor at the University of California at Berkeley this year, where he will teach courses in Indonesian and Southeast Asian culture. Mohamad is the Asian representative on the Advisory Committee for the ICIJ. Goenawan Mohamad's collection of essays, *In Other Words: Forty Years of Essays*, translated by Jennifer Lindsay will be published by Arcade in early 2017.

MARY OTIS is the author of the short story collection *Yes, Yes, Cherries*. Her writing has appeared in *Tin House*, *Electric Literature*, *Zyzzyva*, *McSweeney's*, *Best New American Voices*, *Los Angeles Times*, and numerous other journals and anthologies. Mary is a fiction professor in the UC Riverside Low-Residency MFA program. She is at work on a novel.

HADLEY DAVIS RIERSON'S television and feature film screenwriting credits include *Dawson's Creek*, *Spin City*, *Scrubs*, and Disney's *Ice Princess*. Her articles and essays have appeared in *The New York Times*, *The Huffington Post*, and *Teen Vogue*.

FRANCESCA T. ROYSTER is professor and chair of English at DePaul University, where she teaches courses in Shakespeare studies, performance studies, critical race theory, gender and queer theory, and African-American literature. She received her PhD in English from the University of California, Berkeley in 1995.

WILL SCHUTT is the author of *Westerly*, winner of the 2012 Yale Series of Younger Poets Award. His poems and translations from Italian have appeared in *Agni*, *A Public Space*, *The New Republic*, and elsewhere. He currently lives in Baltimore.

ALEXIS SMITH was born in 1949 in Los Angeles and lives in Los Angeles. She received a Bachelor of Arts from University of California, Irvine in 1970. Honor Fraser Gallery presented her solo exhibition *Slice of Life* in 2013, and her work has been featured in numerous one-person and group exhibitions. Smith is the recipient of several NEA Fellowships, The Rockefeller Foundation Bellagio Center residency, and an Honorary Doctorate from Otis College of Art and Design in Los Angeles.

DAVID ST. JOHN has been honored, over the course of his career, with many of the most significant prizes for poets, including both the Rome Fellowship and the Award in Literature from the American Academy and Institute of Arts and Letters, the O. B. Hardison Prize (a career award for teaching and poetic achievement) from the Folger Shakespeare Library, and the George Drury Smith Lifetime Achievement Award from Beyond Baroque. He is the author of 11 collections of poetry (including *Study for the World's Body*, nominated for the National Book Award in Poetry), most recently the collections *The Auroras* and *The Window*, as well as a volume of essays, interviews, and reviews entitled *Where the Angels Come Toward Us*. He is also the co-editor of *American Hybrid: A Norton Anthology of New Poetry*. St. John has written libretti for the opera *The Face* and for the choral symphony *The Shore*. He lives in Venice Beach, California.

MAIA TABET is an Arabic-English literary translator living in Washington, DC. Her translations have been widely published in journals, literary reviews, and other specialized publications, including *The Common*, the *Journal of Palestine Studies*, *Words Without Borders*, *Banipal*, *Art & Thought*, and *Portal 9*, among others. She is the translator of *Little Mountain* (Picador, 2007) and *White Masks* (Archipelago, 2010), by the renowned writer Elias Khoury, and the 2010 International Prize for Arabic Fiction–winning *Throwing Sparks* (Bloomsbury Qatar Foundation Publishing, 2014), by Abdo Khal. Her translations of Sinan Antoon's *Ave Maria* and Hisham Bustani's *The Monotonous Chaos of Existence* are forthcoming.

KATIE WECH is a television writer and mother of two living in Los Angeles.

MARTIN WOESSNER is Associate Professor of History & Society at the City College of New York's Center for Worker Education. He is the author of *Heidegger in America* (Cambridge UP, 2011).

KIM YOUNG is the author of *Night Radio*, winner of the 2011 Agha Shahid Ali Poetry Prize (University of Utah Press) and finalist for the 2014 Kate Tufts Discovery Award. She is the founding editor of *Chaparral* — an online journal featuring poetry from Southern California. She teaches at California State University Northridge and lives in LA with her husband and daughter.

TOM ZOELLNER is the author of five nonfiction books, including *Train: Riding the Rails that Created the Modern World*. He is the co-author of *The New York Times* bestselling book *An Ordinary Man*, and his book Uranium won the 2011 Science Writing Award from the American Institute of Physics. His writing has appeared in *Harper's*, *The Atlantic*, *Time*, *Foreign Policy*, *Departures*, *The Wall Street Journal*, *Men's Health*, the *Oxford American*, and many other places. An Associate Professor of English at Chapman University, he lives in downtown Los Angeles.

FOLLOWING PAGE:
ALIKA COOPER
UNKNOWN #4, 2016
VINYL PAINT AND FABRIC ON PANEL
14 X 11"

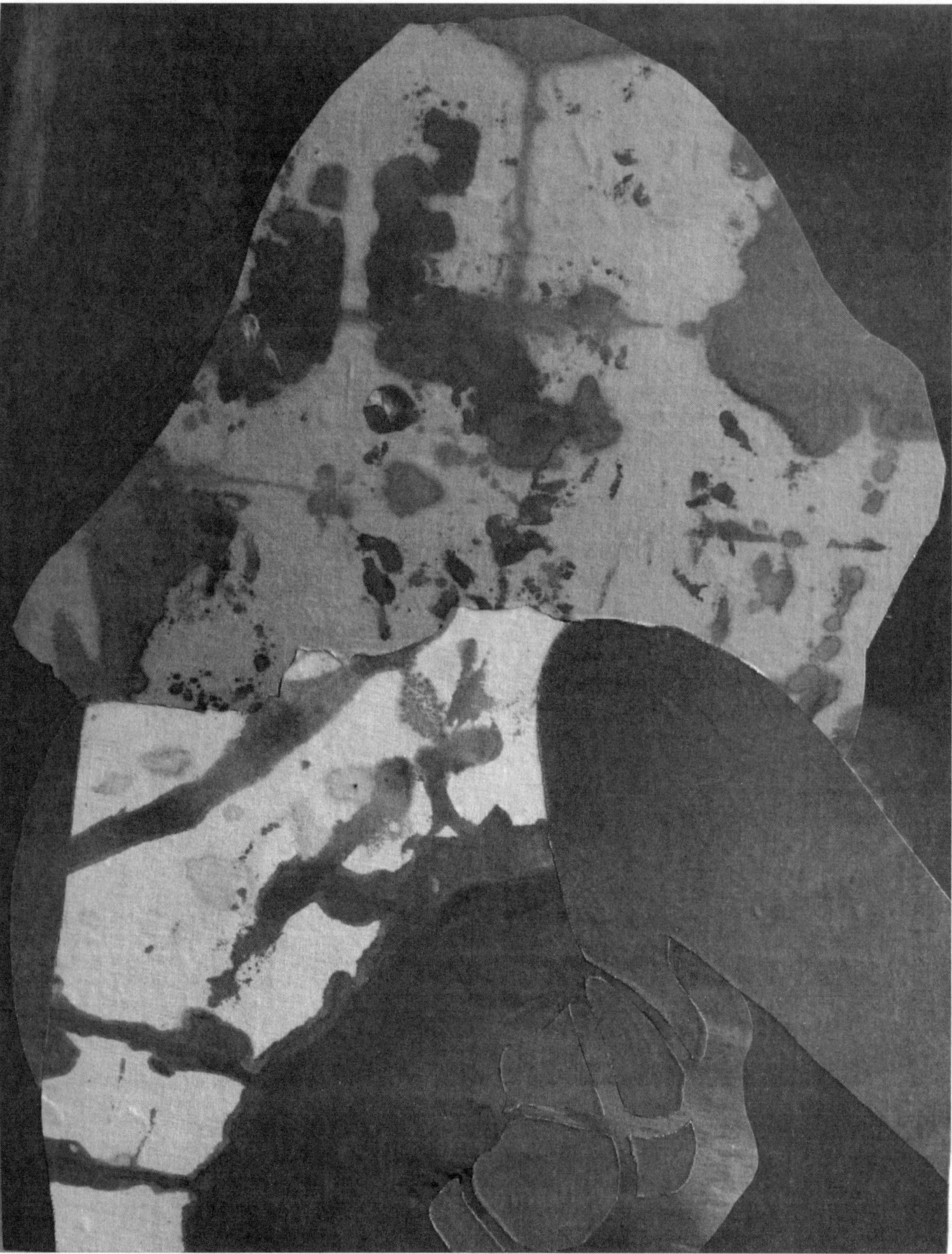